The Morality Gap

THE
Morality Gap

Paul Hanly Furfey

The Macmillan Company, New York

Collier-Macmillan Ltd., London

Nihil Obstat:

> Rev. Thomas J. Harte, C.Ss.R.
> Censor Deputatus

Imprimatur:

> ✠Patrick Cardinal O'Boyle
> Archbishop of Washington

June 5, 1968

The nihil obstat and imprimatur are official declarations that a book or pamphlet is free of doctrinal or moral error. No implication is contained therein that those who have granted the nihil obstat and the imprimatur agree with the content, opinions, or statements expressed

Library of Congress Catalog Card Number: 68-28292

First Printing

*The Macmillan Company, New York
Collier-Macmillan Canada Ltd., Toronto, Ontario*

Printed in the United States of America

To four valiant women

Dorothy Day
Gladys Sellew
Mary Elizabeth Walsh
Catherine de Hueck

*who organized centers of personalist action
in inner-city ghettos*

*who enlightened me and changed
the course of my life*

Contents

Preface

OVER LONG centuries Christianity has been the professed religion of Western civilization. Yet we have failed to build a society reflecting Christian principles. Our society is not founded on the law of love. The present book will deal with this phenomenon.

Part One will defend the thesis that the trouble is largely due to an error of the intellectual order. The Christian code of morality has been altered. It has been corrupted. What we apply to social issues is usually not Christianity but a pseudo-Christianity.

Part Two will discuss the individual Christian's obligation to work for the creation of a better society through personalist action. The techniques of nonparticipation, bearing witness, and nonviolence will be discussed. Through these methods, the Christian actionist can fulfill his obligation.

I have tried to make the book ecumenical in outlook. What is discussed is Christian social action rather than specifically Catholic social action. However, my unfamiliarity with the details of social action in churches other than Catholic has forced me to limit my examples almost exclusively to the latter. Also, although I have little or nothing to say about Jewish social action, let me state emphatically that I am very conscious that church and synagogue share a single Judeo-Christian religious tradition. Therefore practically all of what is said in this book might be restated in Jewish terminology without a great deal of change.

PAUL HANLY FURFEY

Part One

CHAPTER I

The Two Codes

JESUS CHRIST bequeathed to His followers a conduct code of unearthly beauty, a code grounded on love. This love would not only bind man to God, but also to his fellow man, so that human society would become a community united in love. Love would replace violence, and citizens would cooperate willingly, without coercion, for the common good, just as the members of a loving family cooperate. This New Testament ideal, this ethic of love, will be called in the present book the *Authentic Code* of Christian morality. Obedience to this code held out the promise of a new life in a new society, a society of unexampled perfection.

It is all too tragically obvious that mankind has not wholeheartedly accepted the Authentic Code. Christianity has been the professed religion of Western civilization for a great many centuries and has spread in some degree to all parts of the earth. Yet the new and blessed society preached by Christ has not come into being.

It is true that Christianity has had a profound effect on a great many individuals. It has inspired countless generous persons to put aside selfish ambition and to devote themselves to the spiritual and temporal service of their neighbor. Missionaries

3

have risked their lives and sacrificed their comfort to preach the gospel in distant lands. Countless institutions have been founded for the care of the destitute, the aged, the feeble-minded, the mentally or physically ill, and others in need. It is a glory of Christianity that it has inspired century after century of loving service. Many saintly individuals have sincerely endeavored to mold their lives by the Authentic Code of Christian love.

It is also a fact that this code has occasionally inspired whole social groups to guide their community living, as well as their individual behavior by its ideal of love. Such was the case with some of the local communities in the early Church as their life has been reported in the New Testament and in the early patristic literature.[1] They were communities of which it might be said, as it was said of the Christians at Jerusalem, that "the multitude of the believers were of one heart and one soul."[2] Groups animated by such a spirit have reappeared sporadically during the history of Christianity. The early Franciscans, for example, might be cited as such a community. There have been other such groups, too. Yet it must be admitted that examples of such societal perfection have been few and scattered. It would be absurd to claim that during the Christian Era society as a whole has been profoundly influenced by the Authentic Code of love.

No, the disappointing fact remains that Christianity has had very little effect on the ethos of organized society as such. Christian states have handled their international relations on principles not very different from those of pagan states. The Christian centuries have been centuries of war and threats of war. The exploitation of the hungry poor by the affluent rich, the oppression of the weak by the powerful, the mutual hatred of different ethnic, national, and religious groups have been very familiar phenomena in Christian societies. It is rather hard to persuade oneself that in these respects the teachings of Christianity have had a very noticeable effect on the spirit of society and its policies.

4

All this is profoundly disturbing. Jesus Christ called for a transformation of society. Mankind was offered a rebirth into a new and supernatural life. As individuals, many responded and the beauty of the Authentic Code, the Christian ideal, became visible in their lives. Yet society as a whole has failed to respond. A genuine transformation of human society has not been achieved.[3]

One reason for this is painfully obvious. Leaders of the Christian community have often tolerated social evils which were completely contrary to the spirit of the New Testament. They remained silent when they should have spoken out. Worse still, they often publicly approved these evils and participated actively in them. When they approved they were obviously not applying the Authentic Code. They were applying a denatured and watered-down version of it, a warped sort of Christian morality which in this book will be called the *Popular Code*. The gap between the two codes will be called the *Morality Gap*.

The balance of this chapter will give three examples to document the statements of the preceding paragraph. Relevant instances might be found in almost any age of Christian history, but those to be presented here will be three relevant to our own time. They will be three examples of massive evils which were approved by Catholic leaders and in which Catholics actively participated. American Catholics accepted Negro slavery and their spokesmen approved it. The German bishops supported Hitler's war. During World War II Catholics participated in the bombing of several hundred thousand noncombatant enemy civilians. Here were three enormous wrongs, totally contrary to the Authentic Code of Christian morality. Yet Catholics, along with other Christians of course, approved them. They approved them because their thinking was not guided by this Authentic Code, but by what is here called the Popular Code.

The first example to be cited will be American Negro slavery. It is important to note that it is not slavery in general that is

5

being discussed. Slavery at some times and places has proved to be relatively benign. What is here discussed is the peculiarly terrible form of slavery that existed in this country.

American Negro slavery depended for its existence on the North Atlantic slave trade. Without slavery on the American continent, this trade would have had no reason for being. Therefore slavery and the slave trade must be considered a moral unity. To approve the former was to approve the latter.

The North Atlantic slave trade must be judged as one of the most massive and hideous instances of organized human cruelty known to history. The slaves were captured in bloody slave raids in the interior of Africa. They were marched, chained together in long lines, to a port on the coast where they were kept in stockades or barracks until sold for shipment. Very many slaves died by violence, from heat and exhaustion, or from tropical diseases. A "conservative estimate" has it that some fifteen million slaves were exported from Africa during the entire history of the slave trade and that perhaps thirty or forty million others died in the slave raids, during the trip to the coast, or while waiting in port for shipment.[4]

The cruelties of the "Middle Passage," the voyage from Africa to America, have often been described. Here only one fact will be cited to illustrate the inhuman callousness of the process. In 1788 Captain Parrey of the British Royal Navy was sent by the House of Commons to inspect the slave ships then lying at Liverpool. He reported on the disposition of cargo space on the *Brookes*, a ship which he considered typical. He found that every adult male slave was allotted a space measuring six feet long by sixteen inches wide and usually about thirty-one inches high. Women and children were given proportionately smaller spaces.[5] It is hard to imagine the human suffering caused by such incredible crowding during a long sea voyage in tropical heat.

Naturally the Middle Passage took its toll in human life. In 1789 the British Privy Council estimated that about 12½ per cent of the slaves died during the voyage and that another 4½ per cent died on shipboard in harbor before they were sold. The same body estimated that another 33 per cent died during the "seasoning process," during which the new slave was disciplined and taught the arts necessary to make him a salable plantation hand.[6]

Although the importation of slaves into the United States became illegal on January 1, 1808, the law was not vigorously enforced and the slave trade continued on a fairly large scale until the Civil War. Therefore, anyone who bought a slave at any time during the whole history of American slavery, encouraged the slave trade by that act. It is hard to see how he could evade moral responsibility for the cruelties which his act encouraged. It is hard to see how Catholics, even religious communities,[7] could be so morally blind as to buy slaves.

On the American plantation the slave was forced into a mode of life whose effect on human personality can be compared to that of a Nazi concentration camp.[8] He was deprived of his most fundamental human rights. He could not practice the religion of his choice; at most he might attend religious services chosen for him by his master. He could not develop his mind, for it was illegal to teach a slave to read and write. He could not legally marry. His master might allow him to live with a female slave, but this "marriage" was entirely at his master's discretion. The latter could terminate it or he could break up the family by selling its members separately. The slave had no freedom of movement. He could leave the plantation only if it pleased his master to give him a pass.[9]

Thus every plantation was a miniature totalitarian state. The owner could make whatever rules he liked and he could enforce them by severe punishments including whipping, the stocks, and public or private jails. If a slave proved refractory, the master might hire a professional slave-breaker to crush his spirit. Of course, many slave-owners were decent, just men who did nothing to increase the misery that was imposed on the slave by the nature of American Negro slavery itself. However, some owners were sadists or psychopaths who could be exceedingly inhumane. The general effect of all this was to dehumanize the slaves. Deprived of the opportunity to exercise and develop their human abilities, they became something less than men. Here was precisely the essential evil of chattel slavery.

The Christian social ideal is a community dominated by love, a community in which each man loves his neighbor as himself. It is difficult to conceive a system of organized cruelty more directly opposed to such an ideal than American Negro slavery. One would, therefore, expect that all Christians would have repudiated the system in anger and disgust. Yet history proves the opposite. Catholic lay people owned slaves. So did religious, including at least Capuchin, Jesuit, and Dominican priests and Carmelite and Ursuline nuns. The great Archbishop Carroll owned slaves. The Jesuits in Louisiana ran a plantation as a commercial venture; the profit helped to support their missions.[10]

By 1830 a militant Abolitionist movement had developed and the immediate emancipation of the slaves was demanded. This movement reflected the general humanitarian spirit which characterized the early nineteenth century. Until the Civil War slavery was hotly debated as a moral issue. The matter weighed heavily on the American conscience. Under the circumstances one might have expected a pronouncement from the American bishops. After all, it was their duty to lead and guide their flocks when moral problems arose. However, the seven Provincial Councils and the one Plenary Council of Baltimore that were held before the Civil War remained silent on the subject.[11] As individuals, the bishops of the South tended to accept slavery, while those in the North regarded emancipation as an eventual solution for the remote future. In the meantime, Catholic opinion in the North was vehemently opposed to the Abolitionists who demanded freedom at once.[12] There was a considerable variation among Catholic spokesmen, but it cannot be denied

8

that the general trend of opinion was toward the toleration of slavery.

The Civil War freed the Negro, but it did not give him the full political and social equality that justice demanded. More often than not he was not allowed to vote. He did not receive equal justice under law. His segregated schools were regularly inferior. Usually only the simplest and most poorly paid jobs were open to him. To establish interracial justice has required a long struggle which is not yet ended. The role of American Catholics in this struggle has been rather inconsistent. On the one hand there was a tendency to segregate the Negro in special colored parishes and parochial schools; or if Negroes were admitted to a white church, to seat them on separate benches. There were separate sisterhoods for colored nuns. On the other hand, there have been Catholic leaders, such as Archbishop John Ireland and the journalist, John Boyle O'Reilly, who spoke early and forcefully for complete interracial justice, while from 1875 to 1900 the Negro Bishop James Augustine Healy governed the See of Portland, Maine.[13]

What seems unsatisfactory about the Church's work for interracial justice has been the tendency for Catholic thought merely to reflect contemporary thought on the subject and thus to do no more than to move with the times. It cannot be said that Catholic leaders have in general tended to invoke abstract Christian principles on the interracial situation and then to follow these principles remorselessly to their logical conclusion. There have been many contradictions in the Catholic position. When the parochial schools of the New Orleans Archdiocese were integrated in 1962, Leander Perez, political boss of Plaquemines Parish, was excommunicated for his opposition to the decision. His comment was: "How come we could have slaves, separate schools and churches for these Negroes for ages and ages and now all of a sudden it's a sin?" It was a good question. Perez was excommunicated for advocating what had been Cath-

olic practice for generations. The Archdiocese came out unam-
biguously for interracial justice—but only at long last.[14]

The Catholics of Germany, guided by their hierarchy, supported Hitler in World War II. This is a second example of
ecclesiastical approval of an obviously unjust cause. To put the
matter in proper perspective, however, it is important to note
that the German hierarchy showed a commendable courage in
resisting many of the policies of the Third Reich. Both before
and after the outbreak of the war the bishops spoke out forcefully against many Nazi policies that attacked the rights of the
Church or specific doctrines. Thus there were strong protests
against assaults on convents and religious orders, against the re-
moval of crucifixes from schoolrooms, against the euthanasia
program, and against attempts to "de-Judaize" the Christian religion by downgrading the Old Testament.

The German bishops were much less outspoken on social policies which were clearly immoral, but which did not impinge
directly on the welfare of the Church and which did not clearly
contradict specific doctrines. A relevant example is their attitude toward the persecution of the Jews. It is hard to sum up
briefly the attitude of Catholic leaders in this matter. Guenter
Lewy, who has made the classic study of the matter, considers
three periods. Before Hitler's take-over there was a period of
anti-Jewish agitation stimulated by the Nazis and during this
time the Church "did practically nothing to stem the inroads
anti-Semitism was making on Jewish life."[15] During the time
Hitler was in power two periods may be distinguished: a period
of harassment lasting until 1941 during which Jews were
hounded by all sorts of discriminatory laws, and a period from
1941 to the defeat of Germany during which Jews were systematically rounded up and murdered. During the first of these periods the Church was quite active in defending the rights of
Jewish converts to Catholicism, but it "extended neither aid nor
sympathy to other than Catholic non-Aryans."[16] The policy of

extermination replaced the policy of harassment in the summer of 1941 as German armies invaded the U.S.S.R. "By the end of the year 1941 at the latest, the German episcopate was possessed of quite accurate knowledge of the horrible events unfolding in the east."[17] There were, indeed, some public episcopal pronouncements condemning in general language the unjust treatment of foreign races, but "neither the word 'Jew' nor 'non-Aryan' ever crossed the lips of the bishops."[18] In a country with as high a proportion of Catholics as Germany, many of them must have been among those who participated in the massacre of the Jews; yet there was never any direct and official warning against participation. In contrast, Catholics who engaged in duels or who agreed to have their bodies cremated were excluded from the sacraments.

If the bishops hesitated on the Jewish question, they were outspoken in support of Hitler's war. Whereas they objected to policies directly affecting the Church, they had less to say about general moral issues. As Gordon Zahn has well said, "The scope of resistance was most generally limited to those issues involving direct attacks upon Church rights and property or those government programs which in the eyes of the hierarchy clearly contradicted Catholic moral principles. Active participation in or other forms of support for Hitler's wars of aggression were apparently not recognized as such a contradiction of principle—indeed, quite a contrary view is indicated by the tenor of their wartime directives."[19]

World War II broke out on September 1, 1939, with the German invasion of Poland. The bishops lost little time in expressing their approval. On September 17 they issued a joint pastoral calling for wholehearted support of the war effort. "In this decisive hour we encourage and admonish our Catholic soldiers, in obedience to the Führer, to do their duty and to be ready to sacrifice their whole person." There were also many statements along the same line issued by individual bishops in their own dioceses and the Catholic press followed suit. By the middle of

September the German troops had overrun nearly all of Poland. Then another policy was activated. The SS began to murder systematically the country's intelligentsia, the clergy being among the first victims. Cardinal Hlond, Primate of Poland, was able to reach Rome where he reported the German atrocities to the Pope. The Vatican radio broadcast the news. These events, however, did not modify the attitude of the German hierarchy. In personal statements and through the Catholic press they continued to support the war.[20]

May 10, 1940, saw the invasion of Belgium, Holland, and Luxemburg by the German troops. On that very day Pope Pius XII sent telegrams of sympathy to the rulers of these three countries deploring the invasion of their territory "against their will and rights."[21] It seemed clear that the Holy Father regarded the invasion as unjust, but the German hierarchy thought otherwise. They continued their support of the war. For example, a joint pastoral of the eight Bavarian bishops, dated February 25, 1941, contained the following passage: "Therefore, beloved flock, we direct to you a word of exhortation in our paternal love and concern to inspire you to devote your full efforts to the service of the Fatherland and the dear Homeland in the conscientious fulfillment of duty and the serious awareness of your mission."[22] It seems incredible that the bishops could give their blessing so explicitly to Hitler's aggressive war.

When the Germans attacked Soviet territory on June 22, 1941, the enthusiasm of the bishops reached its peak, for it was now possible to look on the war as a crusade against Communism. A joint pastoral issued four days after the invasion contained the following: "The war is demanding of all of you great efforts and great sacrifices. In the accomplishment of the heavy duties of the times, in the hard visitations which the war will bring you, you may be strengthened by the consoling certainty that you are not only serving your country but also fulfilling the holy Will of God."[23] As time went on, and as the possibility of a German victory gradually appeared to be more and more remote, the tenor of the statements of the hierarchy gradually changed. There was less talk about victory and more talk about peace. However, throughout the whole course of the war, there was no wavering in the loyalty expressed by the bishops. There was no hint of any suspicion that the war might be unjust after all or that the military defeat of Nazism might bring certain long-range benefits to the German people.

It is rather disconcerting to realize that throughout the entire course of the war the hierarchy failed to examine the morality of the conflict in the light of theological principles. As Zahn writes: "Nowhere in these episcopal statements does one encounter the question, or even a hint of any question, of whether or not the Hitler war effort met the conditions set for a 'just war.' . . . The German Catholic who listened to or read these messages could only conclude that either the war was 'just' or, if not, that the 'just war' question held little or no behavioral reference to him."[24] It is certainly the duty of the hierarchy to give moral guidance to those committed to their care. In the case of Hitler's war the German bishops completely failed to guide their flocks; indeed, it would perhaps not be too much to say that they positively misguided them.

In spite of the attitude of the bishops, there was a tiny minority of Catholics unsympathetic to the policies of the Third Reich. Often these were organized into small, clandestine groups. Very few of these groups actually plotted revolt. In most cases their members merely tried to preserve their personal integrity by their private rejection of Nazi ideology. Such persons were, of course, deeply distressed and mortified at the passivity of the hierarchy.[25]

After exhaustive research Gordon Zahn could find only seven Catholics who could be classified as actual conscientious objectors, persons who refused military service on the basis of the Church's moral teaching.[26] Of these, six were executed and the seventh was adjudged insane and committed to a mental hospital. It is painful to learn that these heroic men received no en-

13

couragement from their spiritual leaders. Father Reinisch, a Pallotine priest, was refused the sacraments by a prison chaplain in an effort to convince him that it was his duty to take the military oath. Brother Maurus, a member of the *Christkönigsgesellschaft,* was also refused the sacraments until just before his execution. Franz Jägerstätter, an Austrian peasant who was beheaded for refusing to serve in what he considered an unjust war, received direct instructions from the local bishop to the effect that he had no right to take such a stand.[27]

The smallness of the group of those who resisted merely highlights the fact that the vast majority of German Catholics, led and encouraged by their hierarchy, actively supported Hitler's outrageously unjust war.

In December, 1941, the United States declared war against Japan, Germany, and Italy. This action received the warm approval of the American hierarchy: "At times it is the positive duty of a nation to wage war in defense of life and right. Our country now finds itself in such circumstances."[28]

The bishops' support of the war was quite uncritical. There seems to have been little attempt to judge national policy in the light of moral doctrine. Thus there was no sustained protest from the bishops or from Catholic spokesmen against the Allied policy of unconditional surrender, although Pope Pius XII pleaded with statesmen to consider the possibility of a negotiated peace.[29] Father John Courtney Murray considers this the "classic example" of the failure to apply moral principles. For the policy of unconditional surrender "clearly violated the requirement of 'right intention' that has always been a principle in the traditional doctrine of war."[30]

Besides the bishops' failure to support strongly the papal plea for a negotiated peace, there was their failure to protest the American policy of obliteration bombing. This is a point that deserves discussion. "Obliteration bombing," as the term is here used, means the direct attacking of civilian noncombatants by the deliberate bombing of built-up areas. Excluded from the definition is the bombing of military objectives, even though a number of civilian casualties occur as an unintended side effect.

The policy of obliteration bombing was adopted only gradually by both sides. The German air raid on Coventry is sometimes instanced as "the first example of unrestricted bombing warfare"; it occurred over a year after the outbreak of the war.[31] This was followed by similar raids by both sides over the next two years. However, it was not until 1943 that really massive obliteration bombing was practiced by the Allies. The Casablanca Conference of January, 1943, played an important role in the adoption of the new policy. By this time, of course, American air power was deeply involved.[32]

The technique of obliteration bombing gradually became more efficient. During the first years of the war, high-explosive bombs were generally used in attacks on cities; but it was later realized that incendiary bombs were much more destructive. If a large number of these are dropped on a city, a great many separate fires are started, far too many to be controlled by available fire-fighting equipment. The separate fires therefore merge into an enormous blaze which can be overwhelmingly destructive. "Three-quarters of the total devastation brought about by the war was caused by fire."[33] The horrible destructiveness of incendiary warfare is illustrated by the results of some of the major raids. In Hamburg, during the attacks of late July and early August, 1943, the dead numbered over 30,000. Those killed in the raids on Dresden in February, 1945, are conservatively estimated to exceed 135,000. On the night of March 9 and 10, 1945, American planes bombed a three-by-four-mile area in the congested residential district of Tokyo and almost 84,000 perished. In addition to these massive attacks there were of course a great many minor ones, all of which contributed their share of casualties.

On August 6 and 9, 1945, the first nuclear bombs were dropped on Hiroshima and Nagasaki. Official estimates place the dead at 68,000 and 38,000 respectively in the two cities.[34]

15

From the standpoint of morality these raids of course introduced nothing new; it was again a case of the slaughter of unarmed civilian noncombatants. What was new and horribly menacing was the extraordinary efficiency of the bombing. A single bomb could now destroy a city, whereas previously it had required wave upon wave of planes equipped with conventional bombs to accomplish this.

There cannot be the slightest doubt that, by Catholic moral theology, the killing of noncombatants, even in an otherwise just war, is equivalent to murder.[35] This is simply traditional doctrine. When Vatican Council II condemned obliteration bombing as "a crime against God and man himself" and when Pope Paul VI called Hiroshima an "infernal massacre" and an "outrage against civilization," they were merely applying familiar principles to contemporary events.[36] To try to justify Hiroshima and Nagasaki, as President Truman did, on the ground that they "ended the war" and "saved lives," that is, to invoke the principle that the end justifies the means, is extremely naïve.[37] Ironically enough, it would be impossible to justify the bombing of noncombatants during the war even on this incorrect principle. Postwar surveys showed that such bombing was of small help in attaining military objectives.[38] The Japanese were, of course, demoralized when they learned that the United States possessed a new weapon of such horrible potency, but the fact could have been demonstrated without mass murder. A bomb might have been dropped on some uninhabited part of Japan; or, as a group of atomic scientists actually proposed, there could have been a demonstration before a group of United Nations observers on some desert or barren island.[39]

There exists no accurate count of the total deaths due to obliteration bombing by Great Britain and the United States in Europe and by the United States in Japan, but certainly this total amounted to several hundred thousand. It is hard to understand why this gigantic carnage evoked no really significant protest at home. The hierarchy did not withdraw or modify the approval they had given the war. Official spokesmen voiced no criticism. In a democracy where freedom of speech prevails, this silence could be interpreted quite naturally and quite logically as approval.

The Army Air Forces had chaplains. These men were particularly well equipped to pass judgment on the moral issues that the war involved, for they had first-hand knowledge of the conduct of the war and they also had a professional background of training in moral theology. Furthermore they had, as clergymen, the duty of applying their knowledge and their skill to the guidance of the men under their care in accord with Christian principles. Yet, as far as the present writer can discover, they generally accepted the policy of obliteration bombing uncritically. At least it is quite certain that their attitude did not alter the policy. How were these chaplains able to stand aside without protest while the men committed to their care engaged in murder on such a gigantic scale?[40]

The attitude of the clergy on obliteration bombing suggests a very horrifying possibility. Can it be that some Christians simply reject the moral teachings of Jesus Christ when they conflict with national policy? On December 23, 1965, Cardinal Spellman arrived in Vietnam and was interviewed by newsmen. On this occasion he expressed his attitude toward the current war by paraphrasing Stephen Decatur, "Right or wrong, my country." To follow one's country's policy, even when this policy is morally wrong, is certainly to act contrary to the revealed doctrine of the New Testament.

It would be consoling to believe that the Cardinal's statement was a mere slip of the tongue; but, since it received worldwide publicity and was not modified or retracted, it is hard to accept such an interpretation. Moreover, as Dorothy Dohen has shown in a brilliant but disturbing book, the attitude expressed by the Cardinal has been somewhat traditional during the course of American Catholic history. Indeed, Cardinal Spellman himself gave another example of it during the Vatican Council. He ex-

17

pressed himself there in favor of religious liberty, the individual's right to worship God according to his own conscience; yet he also expressed his rejection of the right of conscientious objection. In other words, an individual may follow his conscience, be it right or wrong, in religious matters; but he must obey his country's call to arms, even though he feels morally certain that the war is unjust.[41]

Dr. Dohen gives many examples of nationalistic attitudes expressed by prominent ecclesiastics in the past. It will suffice to cite here just one of these. On St. Patrick's Day, 1861, just before the outbreak of the Civil War, Archbishop Hughes delivered a lecture in which he referred to the looming conflict. Although he did not agree with southern Catholics in their support of the southern position, he nevertheless did feel that it was quite right for them to go to war in defense of that position. As he expressed it in his lecture, "There is but one rule for a Catholic wherever he is, and that is, to do his duty there as a citizen."[42] This was, again, an expression of the principle that the individual's ultimate loyalty must be to his government rather than to the moral law. The good archbishop seemed to be reversing the principle expressed by St. Peter and the Apostles so that it would read, "We must obey men rather than God."

What has preceded makes it clear that the Christian community sometimes participates in massive violations of social justice and that this is done with the approval of spiritual leaders. The examples given have emphasized participation specifically by Catholics; but the history of other Christian churches would probably yield parallel examples. Many similar instances could easily be cited. However, the three given here are sufficient to establish the point expressed early in the chapter, namely, that a very important reason why Christianity has not had a deeper impact on society is the fact that Christian leaders often fail to apply the teaching of Christ to their contemporary problems. Instead they apply an unhappy modification of it, the Popular

Code. It is important to learn more about the nature of this. The problem will be pursued in succeeding chapters.

NOTES TO CHAPTER I

1 This literature is reviewed in P. H. Furfey, "Social Action in the Early Church, 30-180 A.D.," *Theol. Studies,* 2 (1941), pp. 171-197, and 3 (1942), pp. 89-108.

2 Acts 4:32. Here and throughout the book the author has made free use of the standard translations of the Bible. However, he has in each case consulted the original text and has not hesitated to use his own translations when this seemed advisable.

3 It is notable that the Apocalypse represents the Church as struggling with the world, the Kingdom of Satan, and suffering frequent temporary defeats. The failure of Christianity to create a perfect human society as of now should therefore surprise no one.

4 Daniel P. Mannix, *Black Cargoes; a History of the Atlantic Slave Trade, 1518-1865* (New York, Viking, 1962), p. 287. This is the standard work on the subject.

5 *Ibid.,* p. 107.

6 *Ibid.,* p. 123.

7 Roger Baudier, *The Catholic Church in Louisiana* (New Orleans, Roger Baudier, 1939), pp. 108, 121, 145.

8 The point is well made in Stanley M. Elkins, *Slavery* (Chicago, University of Chicago Press, 1959), Part III, "Slavery and Personality."

9 The best description of Negro slavery in America is Kenneth M. Stampp, *The Peculiar Institution* (New York, Knopf, 1956).

10 For details, see especially Madeleine Hooke Rice, *American Catholic Opinion in the Slavery Controversy* (New York, Columbia University Press, 1944), pp. 33, 46-47, 138. See also Baudier, *op. cit.*

11 However, in the Fourth Provincial Council the apostolic letter of Gregory XVI, *In supremo apostolatus,* which condemned the slave trade, was read.

12 Archbishop Hughes declared that the Abolitionists stood "in need of a straitjacket and the humane protection of a lunatic asylum." Rice, *op. cit.,* p. 120.

13 For an excellent life of this prelate, see Albert S. Foley, *Bishop Healy, Beloved Outcast* (New York, Farrar, Straus and Young, 1954).

14 William A. Osborne, *The Segregated Covenant* (New York, Herder and Herder, 1967). This is a very good study of race relations among American Catholics. It adds a great deal of detail to the generalizations of the preceding two paragraphs.

15 Guenter Lewy, *The Catholic Church and Nazi Germany* (New York, McGraw-Hill, 1964), p. 273. Not everyone agrees with Lewy's conclusions, but his work is well documented and seems convincing to the present writer.

16 *Ibid.*, p. 283.

17 *Ibid.*, p. 288.

18 *Ibid.*, p. 292.

19 Gordon C. Zahn, *German Catholics and Hitler's Wars* (New York, Sheed and Ward, 1962), pp. 77-78. Zahn is the standard reference on the subject. The attitude of Bishop (later Cardinal) von Preysing of Berlin stands perhaps somewhat apart from that of his brother bishops. Lewy states (p. 232) that "he carefully refrained from any support of Hitler's wars." On the other hand, Zahn (pp. 119-20, footnote) was not able to find enough material to justify any definite statement on the bishop's stand.

20 Lewy, *op. cit.*, pp. 226-28.

21 For the text of these telegrams, see Harry C. Koenig, ed., *Principles for Peace* (Washington, National Catholic Welfare Conference, 1943), pp. 668-69.

22 Text in Zahn, *op. cit.*, pp. 78-79.

23 *Joint Pastoral Letter of the German Hierarchy,* June 26, 1941.

24 Zahn, *op. cit.*, p. 68.

25 Lewy, *op. cit.*, pp. 309-321. Lewy notes (p. 309) that when the American troops reached the concentration camp at Dachau on April 26, 1945, they found 326 German Catholic priests. Many more had died there.

26 Zahn, *op. cit.*, pp. 54-55.

27 *Ibid.*, pp. 17-18, footnote, p. 78, footnote. On Franz Jägerstätter, see Gordon C. Zahn, *In Solitary Witness* (New York, Holt, Rinehart and Winston, 1964).

28 *The Bishops' Statement on Victory and Peace* (November 14, 1942).

29 See, for example, *Circondati dal Concorso,* a radio address by Pius

20

XII on his Episcopal Silver Jubilee. Text in Koenig, *op. cit.*, pp. 766-774.

30 J. C. Murray, "Remarks on the Moral Problem of War," *Theol. Studies*, 20 (1959), pp. 40-61.

31 Hans Rumpf, *The Bombing of Germany*, trans. by Edward Fitzgerald (New York, Holt, Rinehart and Winston, 1963), p. 16.

32 For a good account of the development of American policy, see U.S. Air Force Historical Division, *The Army Air Forces in World War II*, Vol. 2 (Chicago, University of Chicago Press, 1948-1958), Chaps. 7-12.

33 Rumpf, *op. cit.*, p. 93. The whole chapter is a good discussion of incendiary bombing in World War II.

34 These figures are taken from U.S. Atomic Energy Commission, *The Effects of Nuclear Weapons*, rev. ed. (Washington, Government Printing Office, 1962), p. 550. Many other estimates are higher.

35 A very good treatment, dealing specifically with World War II, is John C. Ford, "The Morality of Obliteration Bombing," *Theol. Studies*, 5 (1944), pp. 261-309. The older theological literature is reviewed in P. H. Furfey, "Bombing of Noncombatants Is Murder," *The Catholic C.O.*, (July-September, 1945), pp. 3-4. See also P. H. Furfey, *The Mystery of Iniquity* (Milwaukee, Bruce, 1944), pp. 165-166. For general background, see particularly René Coste, *Morale internationale* (Tourmai, Desclée, 1964).

36 Vatican Council II, *Constitution on the Church in the Modern World*, para. 80, and Pope Paul VI, discourse at Castel Gandolfo (August 8, 1965).

37 The phrases occur in a letter from President Truman to Professor Cate of the University of Chicago, produced in U.S. Air Force Historical Division, *op. cit.*, Vol. 5, pp. 712-713.

38 "German morale had not broken, as captured leaders proudly pointed out after the war." U.S. Air Force Historical Division, *op. cit.*, Vol. 3, p. 802. U.S. Strategic Bombing Survey, *The Effects of Strategic Bombing on the German War Economy* (Washington, Overall Economic Effects Division, 1945), p. 39, testifies that "the direct effects of strategic bombing on the size of the labor force never grew to significant proportions."

39 The atomic scientists mentioned formed the Committee on Social and Political Implications. See U.S. Air Force Historical Division, *op. cit.*, Vol. 5, p. 710.

40 Before the planes took off to drop the bomb on Hiroshima, the

crew attended "religious services." U.S. Air Force Historical Division, *op. cit.*, Vol. 5, p. 716. Thus God's blessing was invoked for the commission of one of the bloodiest deeds of all history.

41 Dorothy Dohen, *Nationalism and American Catholicism* (New York, Sheed and Ward, 1967), pp. 1, 154-155.

42 *Ibid.*, p. 140.

CHAPTER II

The Catholic Conscience

T H E E X A M P L E S cited in the preceding chapter make
it clear that, at least in some instances, Christians fail to follow
the Authentic Code of Christian ethics, the law of love expounded in the New Testament. Instead, encouraged by their
leaders, they sometimes follow a sort of denatured Christian
ethic which is here called the Popular Code. It is important to
try to learn more about this. What is the exact nature of the
Popular Code? How widely is it accepted? Does it have its effect
only on certain dramatic issues or is it something that constantly
affects the interpersonal relations of Christians?

The investigation of the Popular Code means, of course, the
investigation of the code which Christians actually use in making their decisions about right and wrong. One possible approach, as far as Catholics are concerned, might be to examine
the tables of sins which are printed in prayer books and manuals of devotion as aids in the examination of conscience. Catholics examine their consciences particularly in preparation for
confession. In doing so they try to discover how they have de-
parted from their principles. If they use the tables of sins for
this purpose, then they are using them as a sort of standard of

23

right and wrong. If there exists a certain consensus among the tables of sins, this consensus might be taken as at least a first approximation to the Popular Code.

In line with the foregoing reasoning, the writer decided to study a sample of tables of sins. There being no feasible way of drawing a probability sample from the universe of all the millions of tables of sins now in the hands of American Catholics, he simply took what was available and ended up with twenty-three tables of sins printed in twenty-two prayer books and manuals of various sorts.[1] Whatever its imperfections, this sample was sufficient to provide a number of significant insights.

The tables showed a good many differences in format. Some were simply lists of sins. "Backbiting, slander, calumny, unjust suspicions, rash judgments." Some consisted of series of questions in the first person. "Have I injured (without just cause) the name or reputation of another? By telling lies about him? By exposing without necessity his faults?" Others used the second person. "Have you been guilty of malicious lying? Have you caused ill-feeling by tale-bearing?" The tables followed various orders of presentation. Most frequently they followed the order of the Ten Commandments, the precepts of the Church, the seven deadly sins, or some combination of these. Several were arranged according to sins against God, against neighbor, and against self.

Some of the books contained examinations of conscience adapted to those in certain particular occupations. *The Rural Life Prayerbook* listed possible sins peculiar to the life of the farmer, for example, "Have I been negligent in the control of noxious weeds, to the detriment of my land and that of my neighbor?" *The New Mission Book* had several lists applicable to those in certain occupations, including magistrates, doctors, lawyers, druggists, and those having a hotel, bar, or public house. The great majority of the lists, however, seemed to be directed toward the average or typical Catholic.

In a number of instances the tables listed as sins acts which theologians would not classify as such. The following would seem at least doubtfully sinful: "Neglect of morning and evening prayers, grace before and after meals." "Not cared to hear Catholic sermons." "Profaned [Sunday] by dancing, drinking, or in other ways?" "Have I thanked [God] for the fecundity of the soil? For rains and fair weather? For the constancy of the season?" "Have I taken steps to insure that the family homestead will pass down to successive generations?" The questionable theology of some of the lists is hardly surprising if, as is here assumed, they are expressions of the inaccurate Popular Code.[2]

The tables of sins differed greatly in length. Some covered less than half a page; one ran to over twenty pages. However, the chief difference was merely that the longer lists spelled out the same duties in fuller detail. For example, faults in the relation of children toward parents may be defined simply as a failure to "honor and obey" them, or a table may give a long list of possible offenses, ending with, "Have you neglected to pray for the repose of their souls?" However, the important point is that the longer lists do not introduce any new moral *principle* not implied by the shorter ones.

It seems fair to state that, in spite of the various differences that have been mentioned, the various tables of sins do exhibit a real consensus. This consensus may be conveniently summarized under three categories.

First, there are sins against the precepts of the Church. These include failure to hear Mass on Sundays and holy days of obligation, failure to receive holy communion during the Easter time, breaking the Church's marriage laws, disobeying the now almost obsolete legislation on fasting and abstinence, and others. These, of course, are not acts immoral in themselves; they are merely breaches of ecclesiastical legislation.

A second category consists of sins concerning duties owed directly to God. Here belong such offenses as sacrilege, blasphemy, cursing, neglect of prayer, despair of God's mercy, or a

25

failure to believe articles of faith divinely revealed. Of course these sins are not peculiar to the Catholic code or even to Christianity in general. They are sins which are defined in more or less similar fashion by all the monotheistic religions.

Finally, there are offenses which, in contrast to those in the other two categories, do not have exclusively religious reference, in the sense that they are recognized as violations of proper conduct even by those who do not accept any religious conduct norm. These are offenses that disturb the smooth interpersonal relations which must prevail in a well-ordered society. Such transgressions include quarreling, violence, murder, stealing, lying, fraud, slander, violations of the sex code, and failures in the mutual duties of husband and wife, parent and child, employer and employee. In the tables of sins, those in this third category occupy by far the major share of the space.

A remarkable feature of these tables of sins is their neglect of offenses involving one's duty as a member of civil society. Most of the tables omitted mention of the category entirely. Those that touched on it at all were very, very sketchy. There was one mention of "duty to one's country"; three listed "civic duties" or some synonym. One table mentioned "contempt for the laws of our State and Country." All of these references appear to be too general to arouse one's conscience to specific duties.

There were two references to voting. One was the question, "Did you vote for anyone you knew to be unfit for office?" The other was curious and smacked of anti-Semitism. "Have you voted for non-Christians who attack the Church?" Two lists contained the question, "Have you given alms according to your means?" Somewhat surprisingly, one referred to the duty of lending, rather than giving, to the poor. "Not lent to some in need." There was one reference to race prejudice. Finally, there was a question on civil disturbance. "Have you resisted the lawful authorities of the country, or taken part in any mob, or association to commit deeds of violence, or disturb the public peace?"

The offenses mentioned in the two preceding paragraphs are all those in the twenty-three tables of sins that, in the writer's opinion, could be classified as offenses against one's duty as a member of the organized community. They are certainly very far from covering the complete catalogue of civic duties. The reader must remember that the sins mentioned are the total for all the tables examined. No single table contained more than a couple of these societal transgressions. As said before, the majority of the tables listed none at all.

It is clear that the authors of these tables of sins did not attach much importance to the duties of the citizen toward society. This is in sharp contrast to the great emphasis given to certain relatively minor vices, such as superstition. *The New Mission Book* asks: "Have you consulted fortune-tellers, or made use of superstitious practices, love-potions, charms, horse-shoes, etc.; read, kept, given, lent or sold dream-books, fortune-telling books, and the like?" Could it be that we strain out the gnat and swallow the camel?

Even in the few meager references to civic duties that occur in the tables of sins, there is no slightest hint of one extremely important duty, namely, the duty of resisting unjust laws and national policies. There is simply no suggestion at all that disobedience is sometimes a virtue as it was in the case of the Christian martyrs. If the tables of sins which have been examined do represent some approximation of the Popular Code, then it is easy to understand why German Catholics fought Hitler's war and why American Catholics bombed civilian noncombatants. The Popular Code completely overlooks the occasional duty of disobedience.

The usual examination of conscience consists in the assessment of one's sins rather than one's virtues. That is why prayer books give only tables of sins as aids to the process. Thus the examination is essentially negative. This fact reflects a common Catholic attitude toward the spiritual life which may be expressed as follows:

Man's supreme duty is to save his soul. The necessary and sufficient condition for salvation is to be in a state of grace at the moment of death; but, for a baptized person, being in a state of grace is synonymous with not being in mortal sin. Therefore, man's supreme duty reduces to this: he must avoid mortal sin, or, if he is unfortunate enough to commit such a sin, he must go to confession and have it forgiven. It is indeed praiseworthy to practice the Christian virtues as well as to avoid mortal sin; but it is the avoidance of sin that merits salvation.

The preceding paragraph is not, of course, a correct statement of authentic Catholic doctrine. Later in this book there will be a criticism of the point of view it reflects. Here, however, it is important to note the effect of this negative attitude on the life of the Christian and his activity as a member of society.

If the practice of religion is reduced to the avoidance of sin, then a great part of life is exempted from its influence. For, under these conditions, religion is merely a negative authority which prescribes what one *must not do;* it has little or nothing to say about what one *must* do. Thus a citizen whose religion is of this negative sort will try to avoid the societal vices. He will not bribe a public official. He will not encourage mob violence. He will not falsify his tax return. However, his interpretation of the Christian ethic is such that it does not logically oblige him to take positive action, for example, to agitate for an open-housing law, to fight for equal rights for women, or to encourage the desegregation of the school system.

Another weakness of the position described is that it is often accompanied by an unrealistic attitude toward the Sacrament of Penance. It is safe to assert that some Catholics believe that if they do commit a serious sin, it can, after all, be remitted without much trouble in confession. This attitude can weaken the horror one should feel for sin, for it is looked upon as a spiritual disease for which there exists a quick and easy cure. Thus the effectiveness of the Christian ethic is further undermined.

Of course it is authentic Catholic doctrine that sins are remitted in the Sacrament of Penance. However, contrition is a precondition for such remission and the characteristics of contrition are exigent. It "is an interior sorrow and detestation of the sin committed with the resolve to sin no more."[3] This resolve, the purpose of amendment, must be firm; there must be no indecisiveness. It must be universal, that is, it must be a resolution to avoid all serious sin in the future, not merely the sins confessed. Finally it must be efficacious; this means that the penitent must be resolved to take all necessary means to avoid serious sin, such means, for example, as the avoidance of occasions of sin. Clearly, the Sacrament of Penance can help only those who are very, very serious about self-reformation.

The Popular Code of Christian morality has been described in this chapter on the basis of the examination of conscience as carried out with the aid of a table of sins. Of course, not everyone actually has such a table before him when he examines his conscience. Yet the tables do represent the sort of standard by which the examination is conducted, whether this standard is actually reduced to writing or not.

The tables of sins which have been described are not the only available evidence on the nature of the Popular Code. One can also consider the way that moral doctrine has been taught in Catholic institutions from the primary school through college. Then there are Sunday sermons, Catholic books and periodical literature, as well as oral discussions among Catholics. The point is hard to prove rigorously, of course, but it is the writer's firm conviction that these other sources of evidence confirm the conclusions which were based on the tables of sins.

For instance, the tables of sins indicated that the Popular Code had very little to say about the societal vices, sins that one

29

can commit as a member of the organized community. The other sources just mentioned seem to confirm this fact. How often does one hear it stated that anti-Semitism is a sin or that there exists a strict moral obligation to examine the qualifications of candidates for public office and to cast one's vote on that basis? Above all, does one ever hear that it is the Christian's duty to resist injustice wherever it appears and that on this basis he must resist unjust laws and government policies, at whatever cost to himself?

The usual failure to apply Christian principles to public issues is particularly evident in time of war. Few persons are willing to face the elementary truth that war is a moral problem, that a war may be either just or unjust, and that it is the Christian's duty to refuse to support a war when he is morally certain that it is unjust.

The tables of sins indicated that Catholics tend to view their moral duty as something negative, as an obligation to avoid sin rather than as an obligation to practice virtue. The other sources of evidence seem to point in the same direction. Everyone is clearly aware that it is sinful to injure one's neighbor by larceny or fraud or violence. But how little is said about the obligation to help one's neighbor positively, for example, by pressing for good labor legislation, by fighting racial discrimination, or by working to provide better housing for dwellers in the deteriorated areas of the inner city. The usual opinion seems to be that it is of course laudable to promote these and similar good causes; but there seems to be very little realization that any sort of moral obligation is involved.

It is now possible to understand how Catholics and other sincere Christians can participate in the outrageous injustices described in the previous chapter. These were simply not defined as injustices under the Popular Code.

Those who live by the Popular Code do not question the established order. It is not astonishing, then, that they did not question the morality of American Negro slavery. Of course the injustice of the system was glaring. It was so glaring that here and there serious Christians were troubled in their consciences. Occasionally they expressed their doubts. However, the power of the Popular Code proved so strong that it prevailed in the long run among Catholics, as well as among most other Christians, and they participated in the evil with clear consciences.[4]

It is not in the least surprising that the German bishops supported Hitler's war. They were merely following the Popular Code as it was interpreted in Germany and as it is interpreted in the United States. If Cardinal Spellman could decide the morality of a war on the principle, "Right or wrong, my country," so also could the German bishops. It would be futile under the Popular Code to argue that the German bishops were wrong because they were supporting an *unjust* war; for according to this code the question of right or wrong is irrelevant. One simply dismisses the issue of morality—and obeys.

The American airmen who slaughtered hundreds of thousands of enemy civilians were also conscientiously following the Popular Code. The chaplains who gave their blessing should have known better; for traditional moral theology has always forbidden the direct killing of noncombatants. The chaplains, however, preferred the Popular Code to moral theology. They made no protest. The massacre went on.

The conclusion is clear. The Popular Code is not an interpretation of the Christian's moral duty which can motivate the creation of a truly good society.

NOTES TO CHAPTER II

1 *Blessed be God,* Charles J. Callan and John A. McHugh, compilers (New York, Kenedy, 1925).
Cardinal Spellman's Prayer Book (New York, O'Toole, 1951).
The Rural Life Prayerbook, Alban J. Dachauer, compiler (Des

Moines, Iowa, National Catholic Rural Life Conference, 1956).
A Dominican Mission (New York, National Headquarters of the
Holy Name Society, 1953).
The New Mission Book, F. Girardey, ed. (St. Paul, Lohmann,
1918).
Guide to Heaven (Boston, Boston Type and Stereotype Foundry,
1843).
Saint Joseph Daily Missal, Hugo H. Hoever, ed., rev. ed. (New
York, Catholic Book Publishing Co., 1957).
Marian Daily Missal, with Vespers for Sundays and Feasts, Sylves-
ter P. Juergens, compiler (New York, Regina Press, 1936).
Key of Heaven (New York, Catholic Publications Press, 1939).
My Prayer-Book, F. X. Lasance, ed. (New York, Benziger, 1953).
The Sunday Missal for Young Catholics, Maurice Le Bas, ed.
(New York, Guild Press, 1961).
Saint Andrew Daily Missal, Gaspar Lefebvre, ed., Vol. 3 (St. Paul,
Lohmann, 1958).
Saint Andrew Daily Missal with Vespers for Sundays and Feasts,
Gaspar Lefebvre, ed. (St. Paul, Lohmann, 1958).
Key of Heaven, J. M. Lelen, ed. (New York, Catholic Book Pub-
lishing Co., 1947).
Manual of Catholic Devotions, J. M. Lelen, ed. (New York, Cath-
olic Book Publishing Co., 1942).
Prayer Book for Children, Mother M. Loyola (New York, Kenedy,
1911).
Official Holy Name Pocket Manual (New York, Bureau of the
Holy Name Society, 1914).
Mein Sonntags-Messbuch, Joseph F. Stedman, ed. (Brooklyn, Con-
fraternity of the Precious Blood, 1947).
My Lenten Missal, Joseph F. Stedman, ed. (Brooklyn, Confrater-
nity of the Precious Blood).
My Sunday Missal, Joseph F. Stedman, ed. (Brooklyn, Confrater-
nity of the Precious Blood, 1938).
Manual of Prayers for the Use of the Catholic Laity, Third Ple-
nary Council of Baltimore (New York, Murphy, 1916).
Within the Sanctuary: the Mass (Niagara University, N.Y., Our
Lady of the Angels' Novena, 1938).
2 Joseph X. O'Connor, *A Survey of the Examination of Conscience
as Found in Some Popular Prayerbooks,* M.A. thesis (Washington,
Catholic University of America, 1954), criticizes prayer books for
including in tables of sins acts which are theologically not sinful.

3 "Animi dolor ac detestatio est de peccato commisso cum proposito non peccandi de cetero," Denzinger-Schönmetzer, No. 1676. For a competent short summary of the distinction between contrition and attrition, see P. De Letter, "Contrition," *New Catholic Encyclopedia* (New York, McGraw-Hill, 1966), Vol. 4, pp. 278-83.

4 Joseph D. Brokhage, *Francis Patrick Kenrick's Opinion on Slavery* (Washington, Catholic University Press, 1955), is a good review of Archbishop Kenrick's theological treatment of slavery. The subject is important because Kenrick's work probably represents the most thoroughgoing treatment of the issue by any American theologian.

CHAPTER III

The Authentic Code Is Love

THE POPULAR Code defines the Christian's duty legalistically and negatively by giving long lists of sins to be avoided.
The Authentic Code approaches the matter very differently. It
defines the Christian's duty quite simply as the one duty of love.

It is somehow hard to grasp and to hold firmly the simple
truth that love is the Christian's sole moral obligation. For some
obscure reason, writers constantly tend to redefine Christian
morality in other and more complex terms. Therefore, it is well
at this point to recall the familiar texts in which Jesus Christ
stated categorically and in the clearest possible language the pri-
macy of love.

First, there was His answer to the lawyer's question, "Master,
which is the great commandment in the Law?" The answer of
Jesus was unambiguous: "You shall love the Lord your God
with your whole heart, and with your whole soul, and with your
whole mind. This is the great and first commandment. And the
second is like it. You shall love your neighbor as yourself. On
these two commandments depend the whole Law and the
Prophets."[1]

Then there was the occasion when at the request of Christ a
questioning lawyer himself stated his opinion of what was neces-

34

sary in order to obtain eternal life. The lawyer said, "You shall love the Lord your God with your whole heart, and with your whole soul, and with your whole strength, and with your whole mind, and your neighbor as yourself." Jesus approved this formulation. "You have answered rightly. Do this and you will live."[2] Thus once again, and in quite similar language, the moral doctrine of Christ was stated as the law of love, the obligation to love God above all and to love one's neighbor as oneself.

It being accepted that the Authentic Code of Christian morality simply reduces to the obligation of love, there remains the question how this abstract obligation is to be reduced to practice in concrete acts. The question is not hard to answer. To love one's neighbor as oneself does not mean to cherish him with some vague, sentimental affection. It means to feel the same concern for his needs that one feels for one's own needs. And the motive must be the fact that one sees Christ in this neighbor. The Authentic Code can therefore be stated concretely somewhat as follows:

"If you wish to merit heaven and escape the fate of the damned, go to the inner-city slums. You will find hungry people there. Give them food and drink. You will find homeless men on your local Skid Row; you will find families who have been evicted from their poor homes for nonpayment of rent. Give them shelter. On a winter day you will find little children there, shivering from the cold. Give them warm clothing. Haunt the hospitals and prisons, bringing what help and comfort you can. And remember to treat these beloved poor with kindness and tenderness and respect—no, with reverence; for if you look carefully at these pinched and suffering faces you will begin to discern the lineaments of Christ."

Does this sound exaggerated? It should not sound so to a Christian; for it is merely a paraphrase of the passage in Our Lord's account of the Last Judgment in which He tells what the saved did to merit their reward. "For I was hungry and you gave me food, I was thirsty and you gave me drink, I was a stranger and you took me in, I was naked and you clothed me, I was sick and you visited me, I was in prison and you came to me."[3] There seems to be a disproportion between these simple acts of Christian charity toward the poor and the immensity of the ensuing reward; but, no, charity is surpassingly powerful because its object is not precisely a poor human being, but Christ in that poor human being. "Truly, I say to you, as long as you did it for one of the least of these my brethren, you did it for me."[4]

The parable of the Good Samaritan also proves the identity of the Authentic Code and the duty of love. The context of the parable was a lawyer's question, "Master, what must I do to obtain eternal life?"[5] It was a question of the minimum standard. What *must* I do? The parable itself is a very clear answer. Help your neighbor in his need. Help him even if it means a sacrifice of time and money. Help him even if he is a member of an alien—and unfriendly—ethnic group. To act thus is a Christian's simple duty. He who does less has broken with the Christian ethic.

The saints took the Authentic Code very seriously; this is shown by their treatment of their neighbor in need. There is an interesting study on this point by Mary Elizabeth Walsh.[6] She studied the lives of all nonmartyrs who had died not earlier than January 1, 1835, and who had been beatified or canonized by January 1, 1935, the date the study was begun. There were twenty-five of these, all Europeans. They came from the largely urbanized Europe that developed after the Industrial Revolution. For this reason their example has more relevance to our own time than, say, the example of the medieval saints. The thought behind the study was that, whereas individual saints may have their idiosyncrasies, characteristics which are common to a whole group of saints and *beati* can be accepted as genuine characteristics of the Christian tradition.

A first common characteristic was their deep respect for the poor and the unfortunate. In them, they really saw Christ. Saint

36

Joseph Cottolengo was a priest of Turin who founded an institution, *La Piccola Casa della Divina Providenza,* which was devoted particularly to the care of those unfortunates who had been rejected by all the other charitable institutions of the city. It housed the sick, the unemployable, idiots, deaf, orphans, and other poor persons of various sorts. Whenever a particularly repulsive case was being admitted, Saint Joseph would go to meet him personally at the door, removing his hat as though in the presence of some great gentleman and giving every sign of affection and respect.

Saint Mary of Saint Euphrasia Pelletier, who organized the familiar Good Shepherd nuns, insisted on politeness toward the poor. "Do not make a poor working man lose his time," she used to say, "when he comes to see his daughter. When the evening comes who will give bread to his family? Let us be kind, *very* kind, to the poor."

Saint Joseph Cafasso was a teacher in an ecclesiastical school in Turin, but he was also active in parochial work and in general ministry to all classes of persons in the city. If he were busy and the Marchioness di Barolo, a generous donor, called on him he might refuse to interrupt his work to see her; but if a tradesman or a servant girl came, he would see them at once. Saint Madeleine Sophie Barat founded the Sacred Heart nuns. One day a distinguished visitor asked to see her when she was at prayer, but she declined to see the visitor. Soon afterwards a coal heaver's daughter asked to see her and she at once went to the parlor to talk to the child. On another occasion she refused to see a pious Roman princess because she was too tired; then she suddenly remembered that she had promised to visit the poor washerwoman employed in the convent and she went off at once to pay the visit in spite of her fatigue.

The saints believed in giving the poor the best they had. For many years Saint Conrad Birndorfer, a lay brother, served as porter in the Capuchin monastery at Altötting in Bavaria. One of his duties was to distribute food to the poor who came to the

37

door. For this purpose he took the best beer from the brewery, the best food from the kitchen, and the best vegetables from the community garden. The poor deserved the best; let the community take what was left. When the sister in charge of the linen room complained to Saint Madeleine Sophie Barat that she gave away the best linens to the poor for whom these were too good, the saint replied: "Too good! Too good for the poor! Why my child, I would give them my skin if I could."

The saints showed what it means to love one's neighbor as oneself by sharing their own food and clothing with the poor. Saint Madeleine Sophie Barat once saw at Nantes an old workman hiding behind some trees and eating dry bread while his companions were having a comfortable meal. She immediately sent him her own dinner which had just been brought to her. Saint John Baptist Vianney, the Curé of Ars, would give away a whole week's provision of food, keeping only a few potatoes for himself. He also kept giving away his clothes; his wardrobe disappeared, piece by piece. When nothing more remained in the cupboard, he started giving away what he was wearing. One day he met a poor man with no shoes whose feet were bleeding. The saint immediately gave him his own shoes and stockings. Saint Mary Magdalen Postel, foundress of the School Sisters of Mercy, used to eat coarse bread and boiled nettles so that she could afford to provide nourishing food for the poor and sick.

The saints were not merely willing to sacrifice their comfort for their neighbors' welfare; they would risk life itself. This is shown particularly by their willingness to attend the sick during epidemics. This was before the development of modern methods of immunization. The mechanism of infection was not well understood. The only known method of self-preservation during an epidemic was to avoid the sick. This the saints refused to do. Again and again stories of their heroism are recounted. For example, Saint Mary Micaela Desmaisières, a Spanish noblewoman and foundress of a community of nuns, went to Valencia to nurse the cholera patients there. She seemed to know ahead of time that she was going to her death. This fact, however, did not deter her. She died, a martyr to charity.

It is very important to realize that the saints' love of their neighbors was not based primarily on the attractiveness or congeniality of the latter, as is the case in ordinary human friendships. Indeed, from a purely natural standpoint, many of the recipients of the saints' charity must have been quite uncongenial to them. They included criminals and delinquents, idiots, victims of loathsome diseases, demoralized and unwashed beggars. They had the supernatural insight to see Jesus Christ in them. It was in the light of this fact that they loved even the least of their neighbors so generously and so tenderly.

The clearest and most obvious manifestation of Christian charity is direct face-to-face service of the sort just described. The immediate giving of food and drink and clothing and shelter fits perfectly Our Lord's description of the deeds of the just which will merit heaven for them in the Last Judgment. However, this is not the only sort of charity. He who loves his neighbor in need will not only do all he can personally to help him on a one-to-one basis; he will try to interest others to help him so that relief can be brought to more and more persons. Love, then, should stimulate organized charity as well as individual charity.

Saint Conrad Birndorfer served the poor of Altötting for forty-one years; he certainly accomplished much. Yet just one of the foundations of Saint Vincent de Paul, the Daughters of Charity, now has some 45,000 members serving the poor in almost every country of the world; and the saint has been dead for over three centuries. It would be most presumptuous to argue that Saint Vincent was more charitable than Saint Conrad, but he was certainly more effective. Organization multiplies love.

Some of the works of mercy by their very nature require organized effort. A single lay individual may visit the sick and bring them sympathy and solace. A physician can contribute his professional skill; yet, except in the most trivial illnesses, a lone physician cannot be very helpful. He needs the assistance of other physicians with specialized skills. He needs a team of nurses, technicians, pharmacists. He needs elaborate and expensive apparatus. He who loves his neighbor strives to help him as effectively as possible; and he who loves his sick neighbor does not rest until he has mobilized all the personnel and equipment that a good hospital requires.

There are all sorts of other charitable works that require organized effort. Many of the needy can best be served in institutions, including those for dependent children, for the aged, for mental defectives, for delinquents. Many services rendered by social workers must be organized through established social agencies. Then there are voluntary societies, such as the Saint Vincent de Paul Society. It would be easy to multiply examples.

There is a special type of organized charitable endeavor that is peculiar to democratic societies like our own. This is group action to secure social justice through legislation or through influence on public policy. If it is an act of Christian love to feed a hungry man, surely it is an even greater one to obtain a job for him so that he may become self-supporting. However, getting decent jobs for the unemployed may involve a whole series of activities. It may involve agitation for minimum-wage legislation. It may mean fighting the racial discrimination of labor unions and employers. It may lead to the making available of vocational training to retrain the unemployed. It is unnecessary to labor the point. Christian love does of course involve helping the needy person, either through individual or organized effort. Yet it can involve much more. It can involve elaborate programs of social action to eliminate those social conditions which create poverty in the first place. Certainly Christian love will urge one toward such social action.

Love can show itself also through activities that are primarily intellectual and scientific. In order to help, it is first necessary to understand. To aid the sick, medical research is needed as well as medical service. Crime and delinquency constitute a great and growing problem today, particularly in the cities. Not much progress will be made in meeting this problem until vastly more knowledge has been accumulated about its causes. The old idea that all that is necessary is to treat the offender with more severity can be dismissed as naïve. What is true of crime and delinquency is true of all social problems. A great increase in knowledge is needed before it will be possible to alleviate these social ills. Love of neighbor should motivate one to seek such an increase in knowledge.

It is clear that Christian love must operate through organized action as well as through individual action if it is to be as effective as possible. However, it is important to be aware of a certain danger in organized action when it becomes impersonal. Love of the needy may then be mixed with other, and less worthy, motives.

The executive of a caseworking agency sits in his comfortable office. From there he supervises the activities of two or three dozen clerks and professional caseworkers. The phone rings and he talks to someone in the local power structure, for he is on easy terms with community leaders. Everything around him reflects efficiency. A great deal of thought has gone into agency policies; and these policies reflect a determined and intelligent effort to bring maximum help to a maximum number of needy persons. Is this perhaps the perfect embodiment of Christian charity?

The United Givers Fund is having a dinner to launch the annual drive. The affair is held in a good downtown hotel. The place buzzes with conversation as businessmen, clergymen, social-work executives, and professional fund raisers mingle for a preprandial cocktail. Dinner is served and it is excellent. The

41

after-dinner speeches are brief, witty, and to the point. Everyone leaves in good humor with a firm resolution that this year's drive will be the best ever.

All this is praiseworthy. It is edifying to know that hardworking businessmen are so ready to sacrifice their time and their money to help the poor. They attack the problems of human need with the sophisticated efficiency that they have used successfully in their businesses. This is edifying. Yet is perhaps something missing? Certainly the atmosphere is not quite that of Saint Joseph Cottolengo's *Piccola Casa* in Turin. The atmosphere of the affair reflects a generous willingness to help the poor; yet it does not quite reflect that warm, personal, and deeply respectful love of the poor that characterized the work of the saints; and is not Christian charity precisely such a love?

The Authentic Code demands a love that is both warmly personal and efficient. There is danger in neglecting either of these two elements. The result can be an attitude toward the needy that is warm and sentimental, but unrealistic and inefficient. On the other hand, the attitude can be efficient and businesslike, but coldly impersonal. Neither of these is true Christian Love.

It *is* possible to combine warmth and efficiency. Many of the saints had extraordinary success in doing so. There are also many holy Christians who will never be canonized, but who also succeed in their own degree. There have been lay people, priests, and religious—leaders of large organized movements—who never lost personal contact with their neighbors in need, who never wavered in their kind, respectful love for the least of their brethren. Of such is the kingdom of heaven.

It is pleasant to imagine what life would be like if people took the New Testament seriously as a guide to individual and community living. Of course, human nature being what it is, it would be futile to hope that the Authentic Code of Christian morality could ever be followed perfectly by all the members of society. But suppose it were taken as seriously as, say, the law of the land. In our country today there is a great deal of crime and illegal activity; but crime and illegal activity are recognized as wrong and condemned by public opinion. Suppose the Authentic Code were taken as seriously as that. Suppose it were frankly recognized as the ideal and deviations from it were condemned. A society whose members followed this code even haltingly and imperfectly would be indeed a good society.

In a society founded on Christian love there could be no place for class war and the oppression of the weak by the powerful. In His description of the Last Judgment Christ tells how those who merely neglected their neighbors in need will be condemned to hell. What, then, of those who not merely neglect their neighbors but actively persecute them? Surely their sin is still greater—and by far! In a society which reflects the Authentic Code even moderately well, owners of the means of production would not use them to exploit the workers. Rather, they would use them philanthropically in the best sense of that word. An efficient factory would be regarded as a means of public service, turning out sound products for the benefit of the community and providing a sufficient and secure livelihood for the employees.

To love one's neighbor as oneself means to be just as concerned about his sufferings as about one's own. To a man imbued with this spirit, the existence of slums would be intolerable; for it would be as unpleasant to know that his fellow human beings were living there as it would be to live there himself. In a society influenced by the Authentic Code there could be no deteriorated housing. There could never be hunger, side by side with affluence. There could be no neglect of health care for even the humblest member of the community.

In current American society the rich are separated from the poor by a tragic differential in their levels of living. However, this may not be the fundamental evil. There is a lack of mutual understanding that may be still more basic. The rich and the poor live in separate mental worlds as well as in separate physical worlds. The rich look on the poor as shiftless and unmoral; the poor look on the rich as selfish and oppressive. One effect of Christian love would be the achievement of mutual understanding. When one loves another, one approaches him sympathetically, and sympathy leads to insight. Only persons with such insight are in a position to work out their mutual problems successfully.

Even a halfhearted acceptance of the Authentic Code would render war almost inconceivable. It is true that just wars are possible under Catholic theology; perhaps the Barbary Wars waged by the United States against the piratical Barbary States in 1801-1805 and 1815 would fall into this category. However, even a just war is no excuse for violating the injunction that one must love one's enemy. If force is to be used, it must be used reluctantly. The Christian cannot regard war as a glorious adventure; at most it may sometimes be a nasty necessity.

The spirit of modern war as it is always waged is the very antithesis of Christian love. An earlier chapter discussed the slaughter of hundreds of thousands of civilian noncombatants in World War II. Every war furnishes an abundance of examples of atrocities. At the present writing the United States is waging a war in Vietnam in which tiny children are being hideously burned with napalm and captives are being cruelly tortured,[7] yet protest is comparatively mild and the authorities beam approval. Is this loving one's neighbor as oneself? It is hard to conceive how anyone professing the slightest respect for the teaching of the New Testament could for a moment condone such atrocities.

Today the whole world shudders at the prospect of a possible nuclear war. All sorts of preventive measures are being considered. Perhaps such a war can be prevented by a stronger United Nations. Perhaps there is some sort of treaty which would preserve the peace. Perhaps the United States should build up a massive arsenal of nuclear weapons which would serve as a deterrent. Perhaps some effective defense against nuclear weapons can be developed. Certainly all these possibilities should be explored. Yet the strongest defense against disaster is Christian love. If man could accept the ethic of love in even a feeble way, it would be enough to prevent the inconceivably gigantic act of anti-human hatred which a nuclear war would represent. For the problem of war, as for other human problems, respect for the Authentic Code is the answer.

NOTES TO CHAPTER III

1 Mt. 22:36-40.

2 Lk. 10:27-28.

3 Mt. 25:35-36.

4 Mt. 25:40.

5 Lk. 10:25

6 Mary Elizabeth Walsh, *The Saints and Social Work* (Silver Spring, Maryland, The Preservation of the Faith, 1937). The various examples from the lives of the saints on the pages following are taken from this book in which references to the primary sources may be found.

7 At the trial of Captain Howard B. Levy before a military tribunal at Fort Jackson, South Carolina, witnesses for the defense testified on May 24, 1967, about the torture of captives in Vietnam. The chief witnesses were Robin Moore, a great admirer of the Special Forces (Green Berets) and author of a popular book about them; Donald Duncan, former member of the Special Forces and now a critic of them; and a medical officer, Captain Peter Bource, whose attitude was more neutral. All these witnesses had seen the war at first hand and, in spite of their different attitudes, all agreed that the torture of captives was the usual practice. The torture was not administered by the United States troops themselves; prisoners were turned over for the purpose to groups of South Vietnamese attached to the United States units. Of course, this testimony came as a surprise to no one. Many reporters had written of it. However, if any confirmation were needed, this testimony in a military court furnished it dramatically.

CHAPTER IV

The Futility
of the Popular Code

THE POPULAR Code defines morality in terms of sins to be avoided rather than in terms of virtues to be practiced. However, even in its way of defining sin the Popular Code is inefficient. It defines sin legalistically. Sin is the violation of a precept. The implication is that sin is created by the will of a legislator who forbids certain acts.

Modern moral theologians like to use the term "fundamental option" for the individual's free dedication of his whole volitional existence to God. It is a voluntary choice of God over self. To make such a choice is, of course, the same as to love God with all one's whole heart and soul and strength and mind. It is the Christian's one duty.

The essence of mortal sin is the changing of the fundamental option. It is to opt for self rather than God. The essence of mortal sin is not the external act. It is not quite literally true that it is a mortal sin to miss Mass on Sunday. The intention, as well as the act itself, must be considered. If the act represents a deliberate revolt against God, if it reflects a change of fundamental option, then indeed it is heinous. It is mortal sin. It is the death of the soul. On the other hand, if Mass is missed in a temporary fit of petulance and without much consideration, then the fundamental option is not altered and the sin is not serious. In terms of old-fashioned catechetics, a "grievous offense" is not a mortal sin unless it is accompanied by "sufficient reflection" and "full consent of the will."

Too much attention paid to external acts may seriously warp moral judgment. It is easy to feel smug and self-satisfied simply because one does not do the things labeled as sinful in conventional tables of sins. Imagine, for example, an utterly selfish young businessman. His fundamental option is centered completely on his own worldly success. His life is the reverse of Christian. Yet such a man may avoid all the conventional sins and enjoy a high respectability. Because his pretty young wife is sexually satisfying, he is not tempted to infidelity. He is completely honest because he knows that any dishonesty would be sooner or later discovered and would ruin his career. He is affable with others, not because he loves his neighbor as himself, but because good contacts help business. He may even go to Mass regularly because attendance enhances respectability. He considers himself an excellent Christian because he commits none of the sins listed in his prayer book. Yet he has committed the great essential sin. He has failed to love God above all else.

The type of unjustified self-satisfaction described in the preceding paragraph is particularly easy to attain because the Popular Code is biased in favor of the higher social classes. It does not include the sins characteristic of upper-class life. That is to say, the sins discussed in catechism classes, the sins listed in prayer books, the sins denounced from the pulpit or in the press, are typically the sins committed by the poor rather than the rich. Probably many upper-class people are not even conscious of their faults because these belong to a category of sins which is seldom if ever discussed.

To realize the existence of a class differential in the judgment of sins, consider first crimes of violence. These are characteristically lower-class crimes. "Research in many countries has consistently shown that readiness to advocate and use violence for the settlement of differences between people is more frequent among working class than among middle class individuals."[1] The reason seems to be that in poor neighborhoods there is likely to exist what sociologists call a "subculture of violence." In these neighborhoods, that is to say, the socially acceptable response to an insult is physical violence. People who are brought up in such a subculture are likely to be unusually ready to defend their "honor" by physical attack with or without weapons simply because they have been taught by precept and example that this is the proper way to behave under the circumstances. In the higher social classes violence is frowned upon. Two businessmen may clash verbally at a directors' meeting, but they do not go at each other with knives or handguns.

This is not to say that the higher social classes oppose violence altogether. Far from it. The opening chapter of this book discussed American Negro slavery and the bombing of hundreds of thousands of noncombatants in World War II. In both cases the cruelty and the violence involved had the approval of the respectable gentlemen who set the tone for society. The current torture of captives in Vietnam and the burning of children with napalm carry out the policy of our civil and military leaders. It was not planned by thugs from inner-city slums.

Public opinion condemns lower-class violence, but it does not condemn upper-class violence. The Chicago gangsters of Al Capone's day or the modern Mafia hoodlums are universally despised. They are looked upon as almost subhuman. But Harry Truman is respected as a fine American—Harry Truman who sent to their death those tens of thousands at Hiroshima and Nagasaki. Public opinion condemns violence very selectively. In the language of the present book, the Popular Code lists lower-class violence as immoral, but only lower-class violence.

Crimes against property are usually considered crimes of the lower class. Certainly burglary, shoplifting, pocket-picking, armed robbery, and trading in stolen goods are more common among slum dwellers than among suburbanites. A successful businessman would not be likely to hold up a liquor store or break into a neighbor's house to steal a television set.

From the foregoing facts one should not infer that upper-class people are particularly honest. Edwin H. Sutherland devoted a good deal of attention to what he called "white-collar crimes," that is, "crimes committed by persons of respectability and high social status in the course of their occupations."[2] Sutherland was referring to real crimes, literal violations of the law; but he found that white-collar crimes seldom result in the trial of the offender before a criminal court. If any action at all is taken in these cases it is likely to be taken in a civil court or before some board or commission. Instead of being given a prison sentence, the offender may be ordered to pay damages or perhaps merely to cease some illegal practice. Such offenders are not usually considered criminals. Sutherland created a minor sensation when he called attention to the fact that they were actually law-breakers and that consequently the term, "white-collar criminals," was wholly appropriate for them.

White-collar crime is surprisingly common in the United States. Sutherland himself studied the history of seventy of the country's largest mining, manufacturing, and mercantile corporations for a period of forty years. He found that during that period all the corporations had violated some laws. There was an average of about thirteen violations per corporation. Offenses included "restraint of trade; misrepresentation in advertising; infringements of patents, trademarks, and copyrights; 'unfair labor practices' as defined by the National Labor Relations Law and other laws; rebates; financial fraud and violation of trust; violations of war regulations; and some miscellaneous activities."[3]

Many public officials are in a position to affect enormously the prosperity of citizens who deal with them. They choose the company to be awarded a contract. They choose the firm from which to make purchases. They give or withhold a franchise. They decide to prosecute a case vigorously or not at all. They vote for or against proposed legislation. Under the circumstances there is a constant temptation to accept bribes. If an official is too scrupulous to accept a bribe in the crude form of a roll of bills passed under the table, he may yield to more subtle proposals. He may accept lavish entertainment, a hunting trip, the occasional use of a company plane. The extent of bribery is difficult to estimate because it is hard to discover and prove instances. However, from the number of cases that do appear before the public it is reasonable to guess that the offense is not uncommon.

Fraud is an offense that takes many forms. An elected official may divert campaign funds to personal use or he may charge personal expenses to a government account. Many persons are less than scrupulously honest in preparing their income-tax returns. Insured persons often exaggerate the extent of the damage suffered while claim agents try to minimize it unfairly. A good deal of contaminated meat is sold in intrastate commerce. The public is deceived by misleading balance sheets prepared by dishonest accountants. Fraud is certainly not an uncommon white-collar crime.

Among all frauds perhaps the most despicable are those that injure the health of the buying public. A manufacturer of a patent medicine persuades a cancer patient to use his nostrum instead of seeking prompt medical treatment. The patient dies and the manufacturer is richer. Many of the cruder health frauds have now been reasonably well controlled by regulatory agencies. However, the current cigarette scandal makes the old frauds seem trivial by comparison. The meticulously fair 1964 report to the Surgeon General, *Smoking and Health,* made it clear that smoking had a very seriously bad effect on the nation's health and that it was responsible for many thousands of deaths each year.[4] Since the appearance of the report more and more evidence has been accumulated pointing in the same direction. Yet the tobacco companies have not hesitated to use every conceivable form of misrepresentation to allay the public's well-justified fears; and they have used every form of pressure to resist proposed legislation and the action of regulatory agencies. For the sake of their profits, the tobacco moguls have had no scruple about sending tens of thousands of their fellow Americans to a premature death.

Catholic moral theology has not been very successful in correcting the bias of the Popular Code; in fact, it has tended to perpetuate the bias. One reason for this is the fact that many upper-class sins involve highly complex and technical circumstances. They may concern the workings of a complicated corporation or the intricate network of interpersonal relations in a government agency. Sometimes judgments about engineering or medical facts are involved. Often the theologian cannot understand the problems involved clearly enouh to make sound and certain moral judgments. He is much more at home with simple sins like lying or theft or seduction or assault. He tends to remain with these; thus unintentionally he perpetuates the bias of the Popular Code.

An unfortunate effect of the Popular Code's bias is that it can make the Christian Church appear to be the church of the white-collar class rather than the church of the poor. Suppose a clergyman with no special training and no special insight is sent as pastor to a parish in the Negro ghetto of a large city. He is conscious that theft and violence and illegitimacy are prevalent in the neighborhood; therefore, he uses his eloquence and his power of leadership to guide his people away from these vices.

So far, so good. The pastor is right in condemning the sins of the area and his people agree with his condemnation. What he does not see is that the area people are suffering from daily injustices for which the dominant classes are responsible. The police are intensely disliked because they are looked upon as representatives of the white-collar classes to enforce the will of these classes in the ghetto. People are angry because the area public schools are clearly substandard, because recreational facilities are inadequate, and because facilities for health care are so meager. Men of the area feel a sullen anger because they are not accepted as candidates for decent jobs. The ghetto seethes with resentment; but the pastor is innocently unaware of all this. His is the Popular Code and he is blind to white-collar injustice.

There is a lack of communication between pastor and people. He feels that they are sunk in vice and that their redemption is all but hopeless. They see in him an insensitive representative of the local power structure with no realization of the social injustices from which the area suffers.

Jesus Christ spent little time denouncing theft or violence or marital infidelity. The evil of these vices was evident to all and needed no re-emphasis. What Christ did denounce was the sins of the dominant classes. He denounced the rich. He denounced them bitterly. He threatened them with hell. "How hard it will be for those who have riches to enter the kingdom of God!" This was a most surprising and unconventional statement. "The disciples were dumbfounded at his words." However, Christ did not withdraw the statement or modify it in any way. He emphasized it. "It is easier for a camel to get through the eye of a needle than for a rich man to enter the kingdom of God."[5]

Such language is not often heard from modern pulpits. The relationship between the Church and the business world seems to be rather cozy. Is it merely a coincidence that the white-collar crimes which the rich commit are so rarely denounced in sermons and editorials?

The enormous prestige of the scribes and Pharisees is a good illustration of the class bias of the Popular Code as it existed in the time of Christ. These men were meticulous in practicing the obvious virtues; but they sinned grievously by committing upper-class crimes. "You pay tithes on mint and anise and cumin, and have left undone the weightier matters of the Law, right judgment and mercy and faithfulness."[6] They were so scrupulous in paying tithes on their income that they did not forget to count in the value of the unimportant garden herbs that they raised. But they sinned against the social virtues, "right judgment," that is, justice in general, "mercy," which goes beyond what justice strictly demands, and "faithfulness" to contracts and promises. Their position was analogous to that of the modern business man who sits respectfully in the front pew every Sunday yet underpays his workmen and uses underhanded means to obtain government contracts. The ancient Pharisees and the modern white-collar criminals have both managed to combine extreme respectability with cruel injustice.

If modern clergymen are prone to overlook white-collar crime, they are not following the example of Christ in His denunciation of the Pharisees. He called them "serpents," "brood of vipers," "blind guides," "blind fools," "hypocrites." He denounced them as petty casuists distorting the moral law, as obstacles to the spread of the kingdom of heaven, as killers of God's envoys. He used a striking figure to express the contrast between their outer respectability and their interior evil. "You are like whitewashed tombs which outwardly appear beautiful but within are full of dead men's bones and all uncleanness."[7]

Jesus Christ did not limit Himself to verbal denunciation of upper-class crime. He drove a group of respectable businessmen out of the Temple, apparently on two separate occasions.[8] In doing this He used actual physical force. "He made a lash out of cords and drove all the men out of the Temple, the sheep, too, and the oxen; and he scattered the coin of the money-changers and overturned their tables."[9]

The expulsion of the businessmen from the Temple loses some of its sensational character for the modern reader; the incident happened a long time ago in a far-away city in a building that has ceased to exist. Then, too, the gentleness of Christ has been overemphasized so long that it is sometimes hard to imagine Him being angry and violent. To realize how dramatic the incident was, one must translate it into a contemporary equivalent. Suppose, then, that some clergyman should become aroused

53

at the injustice practiced by a local corporation and that, instead of denouncing the wrongs verbally, he should stride angrily into the company's office and make a scene, overturning desks, scattering papers over the floor, and finally driving the men out of the office with a whip in his hand. It is hard to imagine that such an incident could occur in our day. Yet, if it did occur, it would mean only that a clergyman was imitating literally one of Christ's methods of attacking upper-class sin.

The dominant classes do not accept criticism mildly. Christ alienated the religious leaders of His time, the rich, the influential. They felt that their privileges were threatened. Under the circumstances they had only one possible answer. They compassed His death. Their indictment against Him was summarized in the words, "He stirs up the people."[10] To stir up is to agitate; and it was as a social agitator that Jesus Christ was condemned to death.

Anyone who dares to criticize, boldly and pointedly, the sins of the white-collar class is bound to suffer as a result. Is it not perhaps a bit scandalous that Christian leaders appear so often before the public as the friends and allies of the powerful rather than as their critics? Is not something wrong when there is so little denunciation of white-collar crime even when this crime involves wholesale slaughter and oppression? Father Gillis, one-time editor of *The Catholic World,* used to say that all was not well with the Catholic Church in the United States because priests were seldom, if ever, hanged. Christ as a social critic has too few imitators.

As was mentioned previously, a serious defect of the Popular Code is its negative character. It lists what a Christian should avoid, rather than what he should do. It would not be very illuminating if one should attempt to describe a man's personality by listing the things he does not do: He does not swim. He does not buy General Motors stock. He does not speak French. And so on. Similarly it is not a good description of the Christian ideal to say that one who tries to follow it will not lie, will not steal, will not blaspheme, and so forth. Christ stated His law positively. It consists in loving God and neighbor. It is a positive rule of life.

The futility of the Popular Code may be illustrated by a couple of examples. First, consider the case of a sincere Christian who lives in a harshly segregated Alabama town. He sees his Negro neighbors suffering from all sorts of injustices which make it utterly impossible for them to live a normal life by American standards. What is he to do under the circumstances? The Popular Code furnishes him with a list of sins he must avoid. In his relations with Negroes, as in his relations with whites, he must avoid lying, cheating, assault, and so on. But what positive steps must he take to reduce the rampant injustices toward Negroes which exist in his community? It is very hard to answer this question in the light of the Popular Code. It is very hard to think of any step in the direction of social justice which the man is bound to undertake under pain of mortal sin. There are many things he *can* do. He can write letters to the editor of the local paper or to members of the state legislature. He can contribute money to the NAACP. He can start a lawsuit in favor of some Negro who has been deprived of his rights. He can do these and a number of other things. But what *must* he do? What is, for him, a matter of strict obligation? It is very hard to answer under the Popular Code. As a result the man is likely to do nothing at all. The Popular Code certainly does not encourage social action.

Or consider poverty. In our present affluent American society almost a fifth of our fellow citizens are living in poverty.[11] In less developed countries poverty is, of course, far, far more common. It is the Christian's duty to aid his neighbor in his physical needs. The twenty-fifth chapter of Saint Matthew tells us that those who fail to fulfill this primary duty will be consigned to hell at the Last Judgment. They will be damned because they did not give food to the hungry or clothing to the naked and so on. But how can one reduce this general obligation of helping one's neighbor to practical rules effective here and now? Legalistically minded moral theologians have tried to answer this question by distinguishing various degrees of need, "extreme" need, "quasi-extreme" need, "grave" need, and "common" need. They have talked about the obligation of giving away one's "superfluous" goods. The more one reads these theologians, the more muddied the problem becomes. For, after all, they are trying to solve the problem in terms of the Popular Code—and that is quite hopeless.

The Christian's obligation to act against the problem of racial injustice or the problem of poverty or any other social problem is quite easily solved under the Authentic Code. One simply applies to a specific situation the general obligation. "You shall love your neighbor as yourself." Once a man adopts this principle of action, once he makes his own the bitter suffering of the segregated Negro or the hungry poor, the problem is solved. Without much difficulty he finds appropriate types of action; for love always finds a way. He would now be ashamed to ask how little he can do without committing mortal sin. Rather, he asks how much he can do and he constantly seeks new opportunities for action.

The Authentic Code presents social action as a strict duty, as an integral part of the Christian life. The obligation of loving one's neighbor includes the obligation of taking action against poverty and racial segregation and other social evils which cause the neighbor's suffering. On the other hand, the Popular Code, being negative, cannot define social action as a duty. If one living by the Popular Code interests himself in action against social evils, he does so, not because as a Christian he *must* do so, but merely because he happens to be interested, just as he might be interested in skiing or collecting postage stamps. Since the majority of Christians follow the Popular Code, it is not surprising that only a minority are active social actionists.

It was previously stated that the Popular Code omits the characteristic white-collar sins and that this class bias presents the Church in an unfavorable light. Actually this code omits quite a few sins familiar to moral theology, or describes them inaccurately. This aspect of the Morality Gap between the Authentic and Popular Codes deserves further discussion.

The New Testament is very severe on avarice. Since Christ warned that it is very difficult for the rich to attain heaven, it is clear that excessive devotion to temporal goods is no peccadillo. It can prevent salvation. It can be a mortal sin. Saint Paul went so far as to assert that "the love of money is the root of all evils."[12] Yet avarice seldom appears in the tables of sins. Not many sermons are preached against avarice. People do not examine their consciences on this point. Here is a very important item in the moral doctrine of the New Testament which seems to have dropped out of Christian consciousness almost completely.

Avarice corrupts the individual; it deadens his finer aspirations and orients him toward the grossly material. But avarice also corrupts society. It motivates the rich to exploit the poor. It engenders the class struggle. If our contemporary society is very far from the ideal Christian society, surely an important part of the explanation is the fact that few are conscious that the love of money is a deadly sin. Few are conscious that unworldliness is an exigent duty.

Chastity and its opposite vices form another area where the Authentic and Popular Codes tend to diverge widely, although here it is not so much a case of omission from the Popular Code as a case of distortion. Of course it is not distortion to emphasize the ugliness of impurity. Nothing conceivable is as ugly as mortal sin whether it is a question of sin against chastity or against hope or against fortitude. However, a constant emphasis on one sin with a corresponding lack of emphasis on other equally important sins can result in a distorted sense of moral values. It is probably safe to say that this distortion is fairly common in the popular interpretation of Catholic moral doctrine. Many a person is tormented with scruples about possible sins against purity while he remains quite unworried about the sins against fraternal charity which he commits.

57

Another distortion in this area is the confusion of chastity and prudery. Many persons seem to be more worried about the mention of sex offenses than they are about the sex offenses themselves. A curious instance of this attitude was furnished by a recent article in *The American Ecclesiastical Review* in which the author wrote, "Pornography is at least the equal of any problem challenging Christian responsibility in our society."[13] It is rather surprising that the writer considered pornography to be as serious as the war in Vietnam or the poverty of one-fifth of the nation or racial segregation with all the cruelty it involves. However, the most curious aspect of the statement is that it makes the pornographic description of sex offenses "at least the equal of" the sex offenses themselves. If it is evil to describe a seduction pornographically, is it not definitely worse to commit the seduction itself? However, the writer of the article in question merely reflected a quite common Catholic attitude. It is a very prudish attitude which frowns on any mention of sex. Instead of being faced and candidly discussed, sex problems are to be swept under the rug and forgotten.

Prudery is responsible for a great many human problems, some very serious, some less so. There is the embarrassment and discomfort of the shy teenager who hesitates to leave a mixed group to go to the rest room. Important medical treatment may be omitted or postponed too long because the patient hesitates to discuss with a physician ailments involving the pelvic organs and is reluctant to submit to an examination. However, the most serious effects of prudery are in the moral realm. A problem cannot be solved unless it is first understood. When growing boys and girls are not given adequate sex instruction, they are not equipped to handle the intense emotional problems that sex creates for them. They may be tortured by scruples about nonexistent sins, or they may be victimized in situations which their ignorance could not recognize as dangerous. Every experienced priest can recall pathetic instances of human suffering which

58

could have been easily avoided, were it not for the prevalent prudery.

Chastity involves the frank and dignified recognition of sex as an integral part of human nature which, like all the rest of human nature, is good and beautiful in itself, but subject to abuse. To face all the facts is to do nothing unchaste or shameful. The writer recalls with pleasure the time he spent as a medical student. There was no prudery in medical school, but there was true chastity. There was a dignified respect for the human body and all its functions. There were consequently no oblique references to physical facts accompanied by a knowing leer such as are prevalent in prudish societies. The physician's normal attitude toward sex has much in common with the authentic Christian attitude. Both are frank, unembarrassed, and decent. Both reflect true chastity.

Some parts of classical moral theology contain descriptions of virtues and vices which are based on a quite sophisticated analysis of human psychology. It is unfortunate that these are overlooked in the Popular Code, for they yield valuable insights into moral behavior and the factors underlying it. There is not enough room here to discuss this side of moral theology in any detail, but a few words on the treatment of the virtue of fortitude will be in order.[14]

Fortitude is simply moral courage. The practice of virtue is seldom easy; but occasionally it involves special difficulties, and only the person equipped with fortitude is able to overcome these. For instance, to attend Mass is to practice the virtue of religion. Ordinarily attendance involves no special difficulty. However, to be seen at Mass in a Communist country could mark one out for special harassment. It could perhaps mean losing a desirable job. To go to Mass under such circumstances is not only to practice the virtue of religion but the virtue of fortitude as well. In other words, it requires courage.

One of the subvarieties of fortitude is the virtue of magnanimity, which is a willigness to undertake honorable projects that involve unusual difficulties or dangers. For example, a man might feel called to establish a new religious community of a novel type. He knows the time is ripe for such an institution. In all modesty he realizes that he has the gifts needed for the project. Yet he also realizes that to succeed he must overcome many obstacles, suffer many heartaches, and face an enormous amount of hard work. If, in spite of everything, he goes ahead with the project, he is being magnanimous. If he refuses to do so, he commits the sin of pusillanimity.

Probably few Christians have ever read a great deal or heard very many sermons about the virtues of fortitude, magnanimity and other subvarieties of fortitude, such as magnificence, patience, and constancy or their opposite vices. These are not included in the usual examination of conscience. In the terminology of this book, they are not part of the Popular Code. This is unfortunate. It is probably true that many worthy projects are not carried through simply because the people who should have undertaken them were too pusillanimous to do so. Yet probably few such persons realize that pusillanimity is a sin. Under the Popular Code they did not realize the existence of the moral obligation which they failed to fulfill.

The Catholic Church in the United States is a very successful institution. Its assets have been plausibly estimated at ten billion dollars, which puts it close to General Motors and Standard Oil of New Jersey—and well ahead of Ford. Almost a quarter of the country's population is Catholic. A minority as large as this is bound to be influential. Unfavorable comment from the local bishop can seriously hurt the chances of a candidate for political office. The three hundred Catholic colleges and universities, the more than ten thousand high schools, and the almost eleven thousand elementary schools control a significant part of American education. Almost nineteen million patients were treated in

Catholic hospitals in 1966; thus these hospitals were involved in a good portion of the country's medical practice. In almost every sector of national life, the Church has a significant influence.

Some there are who contend that the prosperity of the Church in this country has been purchased by some sacrifice of principle. Throughout most of its history up to rather recent times, the Church here has suffered from organized attacks by nativists. The Catholic Church, they claim, is un-American. It is a foreign institution whose ideals are alien to the American spirit. To counter these attacks, Catholic leaders have constantly emphasized their loyalty and their patriotism by demonstrating how easily and how naturally they and their followers fit into the local scene.[15] While doing this they have been careful not to say much about those Catholic moral principles which might prove unacceptable to their fellow citizens. Two examples of this policy were discussed in the first chapter of this book. These were, first, the failure of Catholic leaders to condemn American Negro slavery and the slave trade, and, secondly, their silence on the policy of unconditional surrender and the bombing of noncombatants during World War II.

It is interesting to speculate what might have happened if Catholics had applied their moral principles more vigorously. Suppose, for example, that from the first, Catholics in America had condemned slavery and the slave trade and had completely refused to participate in the system. In other words suppose they had dared to be fathful to their own principles. If this was too much to expect, suppose they had tolerated the system itself, but had at least insisted that its evils be mitigated. They might have condemned the Atlantic slave trade and insisted that the laws eventually passed against it be enforced vigorously. They might have insisted that slaves, though remaining slaves, be assured of their fundamental human rights, the right to practice the religion of their choice, the right to legally recognized mar-

61

riage, the right to improve their minds by some education. They might have called for legal codes to protect slaves from physical abuse by their masters. Even a moderate program like this would have been a triumph.[16]

Of course, a vigorous Catholic antislavery program would have given the enemies of the Church an issue. It might have provoked persecution. In 1835 Bishop England of Charleston opened a school for free Negroes. One might think that this was a rather harmless move. Certainly it had no direct bearing on slavery. Yet Bishop England was immediately accused of abolitionist leanings and his personal safety was jeopardized as well as the safety of his Cathedral. The school was promptly closed and the affair blew over. Bishop England himself became very tolerant of slavery and his attitude influenced his brother bishops in the same direction. However, the incident shows the likelihood that a vigorous antislavery program might have made a good deal of trouble for the Church. It might even have produced martyrs.

On the other hand, if Catholics had shown from the first that they could not conscientiously accept slavery, it is conceivable that thoughtful men would have respected the attitude. This was more or less the experience of the Quakers. Even in the South they opposed slavery. As early as 1787 the yearly meetings in Virginia, Maryland, and North Carolina had given their members the choice of freeing their slaves or being expelled from the Society. In North Carolina they worked for the manumission of slaves, they aided freedmen to leave the state, and they helped educate free Negroes. Some Quakers migrated to the North where their principles were less unacceptable.

Of course it is really irrelevant to ask whether antislavery activity by Catholics would have brought persecution or whether, like the Quakers, they would have largely escaped it. The moral law must be followed at any cost. It must be put above life itself. By silence, by compromise, the bishops of the slave states managed to ingratiate themselves with their fellow citizens; but the memory of their achievement is not a glorious memory.

It is unfortunate that the American hierarchy has exerted so little moral leadership in time of war. As spiritual leaders of a large minority of Americans, they could have accomplished much. First of all, at least after the lesson of World War I, it should have been apparent that Catholics needed instruction on the morality of war. Suppose that Church leaders had acted in response to this need. If the classical doctrine on the requirements for a just war had been taught insistently from the elementary school to the university and had been expounded in the pulpit, Catholics would have been able to approach the moral problems of World War II much more intelligently.

When, on November 14, 1942, the bishops of the United States issued their "Statement on Victory and Peace," their first annual statement after the outbreak of the war, they failed to make any reference to the moral issues involved. It would seem that a golden opportunity was missed to stress the point that the state is not above morality and that the prosecution of a war is subject to moral norms, precisely like any other human activity.[17] This silence, together with the bishops' enthusiastic support of the war, might easily have suggested to a careless reader that one would be justified in supporting the war effort of one's country, be it right or be it wrong.

On the night of May 16 and 17, 1943, the British bombed the Ruhr dams and some twelve hundred civilians were drowned. During July and August, 1943, the British and Americans killed more than thirty thousand in Hamburg. There was no protest from the Catholic hierarchy over this very clear example of the use of immoral means of warfare and the bloody slaughter went on. Later, as the Allies appeared more and more certain to win, the possibility of a negotiated peace became apparent. The Holy Father had called for such a peace.[18] However, Roosevelt and the other Allied leaders had refused to consider such a possibility. Catholic leaders lined up solidly with Roosevelt and against the Holy Father; and the war, with its tragic loss of life, continued.

If the hierarchy had merely applied known and admitted

63

Catholic principles to the war, many, many lives might have been saved. The bombing of noncombatants was actually not a great help toward attaining military objectives. If there had been an angry protest from Catholics, it is quite possible that the practice might at least have been restricted by the military. It certainly would not have injured the Allied cause to have probed the possibility of a negotiated peace. Perhaps all legitimate Allied objectives could have been attained without prolonging the war to the point of unconditional surrender. If American Catholics had campaigned vigorously for such a peace, perhaps their action would have had some effect.

With assets of ten billion dollars, the Catholic Church in the United States has been a huge financial success; but has it been equally successful in inducing men to guide the public life of our society by the New Testament law of love?

NOTES TO CHAPTER IV

1 Daniel Glaser and others, *The Violent Offender* (Washington, Government Printing Office, 1966), p. 14.
2 Edwin H. Sutherland, *Principles of Criminology,* 5th ed., rev. by Donald R. Cressey (Philadelphia, Lippincott, 1955), p. 40.
3 *Ibid.,* p. 41.
4 *Smoking and Health; Report of the Advisory Committee to the Surgeon General of the Public Health Service* (Washington, Government Printing Office, 1964).
5 Mk. 10:23-24.
6 Mt. 23:23.
7 Mt. 23, passim.
8 There seem to have been two such incidents. In Jn. 2:13-22, the event is clearly associated with the first Passover of the public ministry of Christ. The Synoptics (Mt. 21:12-13; Mk. 11:15-18; Lk. 19:45) tell of another event associated with the Passover just before the Passion. The timing seems so clear that it is hard to accept the view of some commentators that all four accounts refer to the same incident.

9 Jn. 2:15.

10 Lk. 23:5.

11 For more information on the extent of poverty in the United States, see P. H. Furfey, *The Respectable Murderers* (New York, Herder and Herder, 1966), Chap. 5 and Appendix.

12 1 Tim. 6:10.

13 *American Ecclesiastical Rev.* (July, 1966), p. 11.

14 See, for example, Saint Thomas on the virtue of fortitude, *Summa th.*, IIaIIae, QQ., pp. 123-140.

15 See Dorothy Dohen, *Nationalism and American Catholicism* (New York, Sheed and Ward, 1967).

16 This is more or less what happened in Latin America where the influence of the Church mitigated the evils of slavery for centuries without abolishing the system. On this, see Stanley M. Elkins, *Slavery* (Chicago, University of Chicago Press, 1954), pp. 63-70.

17 Some Catholics, taking a more radical stand, condemned American participation in the war as morally unjustified. Although this is the position of the present writer, he will not urge the matter here.

18 See, for example, the statements of Pius XII, *In Questo Giorno di Santa* (December 24, 1939), and *Circondati dal Concorso* (May 13, 1942). For text, see *Principles for Peace*, Harry C. Koenig, ed. (Washington, National Catholic Welfare Conference, 1943), pp. 632-640 and 766-774.

CHAPTER V

The Triumph of the Mores

IT IS now quite clear why the moral teachings of Jesus Christ have had so little effect on our society. Christians simply have not accepted these teachings as the norm for their societal relations. This does not mean merely that individual Christians have been lax in applying the New Testament code of love in their own lives. It means that Church leaders, including national hierarchies, have often actively encouraged social evils and have personally participated in them.

This book has emphasized three examples of Christian encouragement of massive wrongs, the acceptance of slavery by American Catholics, the approval of Hitler's war by the German hierarchy, and the approbation of obliteration bombing during World War II. Of course, these are not isolated instances. During the history of Christianity there have been many, many cases of ecclesiastical approval of immoral social policies. One has only to think of Christian religious persecution, the slaughter of Protestants by Catholics and of Catholics by Protestants, all with the hearty endorsement of the respective religious leaders.[1] Then there was the abuse of power by bishops and popes who used the prestige of their sacred office to encourage aggressive wars, to uphold the oppressive policies of the rich and powerful, or to enhance their own personal power and prestige. It is indeed easy to multiply examples of the ecclesiastical approbation of social policies which contradict the whole spirit of the New Testament.

In the abstract it seems strange that anyone professing Christian principles should reject them in matters of social policy in favor of something as mean and tawdry as the ethos of worldliness. By the very fact of professing Christianity one commits oneself to the ethics of the New Testament. In the case of a clergyman this commitment becomes a full-time vocation. The churches represent a formal joint effort to guide the lives of their members in accordance with the Authentic Code of Christian love. Church members are acutely conscious of the beauty of the ideal they have chosen. Yet, in spite of all this, in matters of social policy, earnest Christians are prone to reject their own ideals and to follow blindly the nasty policies of the worldly. Why is this?

In attempting to answer, one must not overlook the coercive effect of community custom. Sociologists talk of the "mores."[2] These are standard ways of acting which are considered proper or correct or right. He who observes the mores is considered respectable; he is a good citizen. He who rejects them is punished in various ways. A man removes his hat on entering a house; otherwise he will be considered rude. An employee comes to work on time, obeys orders, and does his job efficiently; otherwise he will be discharged or at least he will not be promoted. A citizen pays his income tax; otherwise he will be heavily fined or perhaps jailed.

It would be a mistake to look on the mores of a society as a set of unrelated and arbitrary rules. Actually the mores define a way of life. They reflect the society's characteristic ideal and constitute a code of ethics focused on that ideal. To follow the mores, then, is to make oneself into the sort of citizen that this society holds in honor.

67

Slavery was not an accidental or extrinsic feature of the Old South. Economically, socially, politically, it was deeply embedded in the regional culture. It was part of a way of life, a form of gracious living which men had loved for generations. To advocate abolitionism, therefore, was not to propose an isolated reform. It was to reject the regional ethics. It was to try to shatter a life ideal which men found satisfying. It is easy to understand why men in the slave states reacted so angrily to criticism.

The Third Reich was a political entity, a totalitarian state with its definite organization. But it was more than that. It was a new ethics. It was a new way of living that had to be accepted by the citizen with all that it implied. To revolt against Hitler was therefore more than a mere political revolt. It was a sort of blasphemy against the special ideal which the whole Nazi ideology represented and for the furtherance of which the whole Nazi state was organized.

There seems to be no abstract reason why the mores of a community should not represent a high moral standard. Historically, however, this seldom seems to be the case. The mores tend regularly to set a standard of public morality which is lower than the standard of individual morality which average citizens set for themselves. No decent man would use violence to seize his neighbor's property; yet he will very probably follow the mores in supporting an unjust aggressive war to seize territory belonging to a neighboring state. No decent man would exploit the weakness of an individual to deprive him of the fruits of his labor; yet he may unhesitatingly support an economic system that does precisely that.

The gap between a society's mores and the Authentic Code is likely to be very wide because the moral standard represented by the latter is so high. Of course, where this gap exists, the Christian's duty is very clear. He must guide his conduct by the Authentic Code of the New Testament, no matter what the cost to himself may be. To do less is to cease to be a Christian, for it is of the very essence of Christianity that it must be the supreme norm of conduct for those who profess it.

To defy the mores and follow one's conscience may demand the most extreme heroism, the heroism of the martyrs. It is a glorious fact that during the history of Christianity many have exhibited such heroism and have died rather than disobey the Authentic Code. Most of them died rather than renounce their loyalty to the Church as an organization and a way of life, but there were also many who died because they refused to perform some specific immoral act. Thus Saint Maria Goretti was stabbed to death by a neighbor because she repulsed his sexual advances, and the cause of the execution of the Martyrs of Uganda was basically their refusal to submit to the homosexual demands of their ruler.

In connection with the present discussion a particularly interesting case is that of the Austrian peasant, Franz Jägerstätter, who has been mentioned already. He, too, was put to death not for refusing to renounce his religion, but for refusing a specific act, namely, induction into Hitler's army. For this refusal he was beheaded on August 9, 1943. The Church has not yet moved to honor Jägerstätter by beatification or canonization. He is nevertheless an excellent example of Christian fidelty to the Authentic Code. While the hierarchy compromised and supported an immoral war, this poorly educated peasant saw the issue clearly and proved uncompromising.[3]

Human nature being what it is, it is perhaps not hard to understand why the Jägerstätters are rare. It requires extreme courage to die for one's convictions. What is harder to understand is why so few are willing to bear witness when the sacrifice required is much less serious, or even when it is no more than rather trifling. To the eternal credit of our country, provisions for conscientious objection were quite liberal during World War II. There were probably more than 50,000 who either claimed complete exemption from military service or who were willing to perform only noncombatant duties. Some 6,000 men were sentenced to prison as draft delinquents, but only a part of them were conscientious objectors who failed to obtain recognition for their status.[4] It seems fair to conclude that the United States, in sharp contrast to the Third Reich, frankly recognized the right of the individual to refuse to obey orders contrary to his conscience.

In view of the intelligent and liberal attitude of the United States Government, it is hard to understand why there was so little Catholic protest against immoral national policies during World War II. Why was there so little criticism of the wholesale bombing of noncombatants? Why was there so little support of the papal policy of negotiated peace? One may perhaps understand the dilemma of the German bishops; if they had protested Hitler's war, they would probably have faced the concentration camp. If their attitude was inexcusable, it was at least understandable. But how account for the attitude of the bishops and of other Catholic leaders in this country? If they had protested the massacre of noncombatants, they would not have been persecuted. In the long run, they would probably have been respected for their action. Somehow or other, the urge to conform to the mores can prove overwhelmingly powerful.

Cowardice does not seem to be an adequate explanation for the failure of many to follow the Authentic Code in defiance of the mores. Cowardice may indeed explain the actions of some. There are doubtless individuals who see their duty, but fail to perform it. However, it is clear that many who accept the immoral mores are upright and brave. Archbishop Carroll was a man of heroic stature, yet he held slaves. Among the German bishops who supported an immoral war, there were men of outstanding character, men who were anything but timid. Our own national Catholic leaders during World War II included many who won respect for their clear thinking and their refusal to yield to pressure on many issues.

If persons fail to protest when they should protest, if they obey when they should disobey, it is plausible that the explanation is to be found more often in self-deception than in lack of courage. The human capacity for self-deception is extraordinary. There are numerous ways of deceiving one's conscience and persuading oneself that a certain duty does not exist, when in fact it does. All this is familiar to directors of conscience. They know by experience that realistic self-knowledge is very difficult to attain and that even a serious and earnest person may have grave faults of which he is quite unaware. The experience of psychiatrists and clinical psychologists confirms all this. They have even catalogued the various techniques of self-deception as "parataxes" or "mental mechanisms."[5]

Self-deception is made possible by the fact that mental content exists on different levels. First there is consciousness—or the *conscious* to give it its technical name—that is, the material about which one is actually thinking at the moment. Then there is the *foreconscious* (also called preconscious or subconscious), that mental content which may easily be brought into consciousness, although it is not present in consciousness at the moment. Thus one may easily bring to mind one's telephone number or birth date; these are normally in the foreconscious. It is certain that there also exists mental content of which the possessor is totally unaware and which cannot be brought into consciousness except by special effort or the use of certain technical methods. This is called the *unconscious*.

A great deal of modern dynamic psychology rests on the fact that the unconscious not only exists, but also can influence conduct.[6] To anyone who has seriously observed human behavior, this is not so surprising, after all; for it merely means that a person may not be aware of his true motives and this fact is familiar enough. This fact has direct relevance to the problem now being considered. For example, a citizen may suspect that the war his country is waging is an unjust war and that it is his duty to oppose it. However, opposition would bring him swift retribu-

71

tion. Therefore, he buries his suspicions in his unconscious, persuading himself that the war is just, after all, and that it deserves his support. This, however, is obviously not his real motive for aiding the war effort. His real motive, buried in his unconscious, is fear of the consequences of withdrawing his support. The man has deadened his conscience and has persuaded himself that he is acting morally when this is not actually the case.

A very direct method of avoiding an unpleasant fact is simply to put it out of one's mind. This is the mechanism of *suppression* (partial forgetting) or *repression* (complete forgetting). Human beings have a curious ability to forget unpleasant facts, even those that are very patent and very emotionally charged. One relevant example in the tendency to overlook the moral aspects of war. In the abstract it certainly seems strange that persons could participate in an activity so dramatic and so overwhelmingly destructive without asking whether it is right or wrong. Yet the attitude is common enough.

During World War II there was a certain amount of moral concern at the grass-roots level. As stated earlier, over 50,000 men applied for exemption on moral grounds. Doubtless there were many thousands of others who also considered the problem seriously but reached a different conclusion, namely, that it was their duty to serve. However, moral issues were seldom raised by religious leaders or discussed in the religious press. It is interesting to browse in the bound volumes of diocesan newspapers or Catholic periodicals published during the war years; one finds remarkably little on the morality of the conflict.

The most dramatic event of the whole war was, of course, the dropping of the bomb at Hiroshima. One might have expected that the moral aspects of this gigantic slaughter would have dominated the comment. This was far from being the case. An editorial in *The Catholic World* summarizes the reaction: "For days and weeks after the dropping of the first atomic bomb on Japan, there was a landslide of comment, scientific, pseudo-scientific and fantastic, opinions, explanations, rejoicing, and even of thanksgiving to God. Somewhere in the enormous mass of matter dislodged, as it were, by the bomb, there may have been a moral judgment, apart from the Pope's. If so, I confess I did not find it, though I searched diligently."[7]

Sometimes the morality of a war is not merely overlooked but is positively distorted. In an earlier chapter it was mentioned that Cardinal Spellman once settled the moral problem of the Vietnam war to his own satisfaction by paraphrasing Decatur: "Right or wrong, my country." This was clearly an explicit repudiation of Christian morality as the supreme norm of conduct. Yet one may be sure that the Cardinal was unaware of this repudiation. Doubtless he simply repressed the thought that Decatur's principle was the negation of Christian moral doctrine. Thus he was able to agree with the superpatriots without being conscious of any disloyalty to Catholic teaching. The attitude is doubtless quite common. In wartime, without doubt many Catholics follow the principle that whatever the government commands is the citizen's duty, and they follow this principle without being consciously disloyal to the moral teaching of their Church.[8]

Another mechanism of self-deception is *rationalization;* this means explaining away unpleasant facts through fallacious reasoning. A prime example of rationalization in the social area is the use of all sorts of sophistry to justify the evils of slavery and, later, the evils of racial discrimination. The bulk of the proslavery arguments began with the false premise that Negroes are intrinsically inferior to whites. They lack the ability to function as free citizens in a democratic society. It is therefore just that they should live in slavery under the tutelage of white masters. The arrangement ensures them lifetime security and physical care which they would not be able to obtain through their own efforts in a competitive community. Although the life of the slave has its disadvantages, it nevertheless represents a step upward from the "savagery" of Africa. Of course, all this is nonsense; but it was taken seriously by the slaveholders. After emancipation somewhat similar reasoning was used to justify a wide variety of discriminatory practices that infringed on the rights of Negroes as citizens.

In an interesting essay, Sterling A. Brown shows how the rationalizations just mentioned have become a part of the American literary tradition.[9] Citing many examples, he enumerates the stereotypes that constantly recur in novels, short stories, essays, and poetry. There are, for instance, the stereotypes of the contented slave and the wretched freeman. Life on the plantation is pictured as idyllic. Slaves were carefree and contented under their kindly masters. Their labor was light and food abundant. Freedom did not improve the Negro's lot. The freeman lived miserably in the white community. Particularly after emancipation, the stereotype of the brute Negro became popular. The former docile slave, now freed from restraint, became a terrifying menace. Luckily the noble Ku Klux Klan was able to save white society. In still another stereotype the Negro is presented as comic. This has served a double purpose. If the plantation slave is shown as always mirthful, then slavery could not have been so bad. On the other hand, the Negro after Emancipation is often presented as a buffoon. He makes himself ridiculous by trying to practice law or to wear a dress suit, which are obviously white prerogatives. It is clearly out of the question to think of equality between white persons and such comic characters. It is worth noting that the Negro is not the only minority group that has been caricatured in literature. All the various minority groups have suffered in turn; among them, probably the Irish have suffered most.

The literary caricatures of minority groups have a very sinister effect. A cleverly written work of fiction can make a very vivid and lasting impression on the reader. For example, if Negroes are pictured over and over again as being characteristically irresponsible, then the reading public is likely to accept their irresponsibility as a known truth. The reader who has little social contact with Negroes is not in a position to check this theory against the facts. If he happens to meet a Negro who is obviously not irresponsible, he may consider this an "exception" which does not invalidate the general rule. Literature can thus build up a vast mass of misinformation which provides false premises for the rationalizations by which the general public deceives itself and avoids the duty of righting social injustices.

Before emancipation, Catholic moral theologians devoted a considerable amount of attention to slavery as a moral problem and their conclusions were generally favorable to the system. However, in reaching their conclusions, the theologians were often guilty of using the term "slavery" ambiguously. When they asserted, correctly, that slavery is not contrary to the natural law, they took the term to mean the system under which the slave gives his master a lifetime of labor in return for a lifetime of maintenance. Thus understood, slavery deprives the slave of no right except the right to change his employer. He retains all his other normal human rights, the right to practice his religion, the right to marry, the right to improve his mind, the right to disobey immoral orders, and other such rights. Moreover, the master must respect the slave's dignity as a human being; he must not make unreasonable demands or subject him to any sort of inhumane treatment. Even thus understood, slavery is an undesirable arrangement. It is easily subject to abuse; and, historically, such abuse has almost invariably accompanied it. However, it cannot be said that this sort of slavery is evil in itself.

It is clear from what was said in an earlier chapter that slavery as defined in the foregoing paragraph has little in common with slavery as it existed in this country. Here slaves were regarded as property and, as has been explained already, they were denied most of their fundamental human rights. Slavery of this sort could not possibly be morally justified. When theologians asserted that "slavery" was not contrary to the natural law and that, therefore, they could not condemn "slavery" as it existed in America, they were using the term in two very different senses—a very clear logical fallacy. The same error was committed by those who cited the biblical toleration of "slavery" as a justification for "slavery" in this country. Again the term was used ambiguously, in two different senses. These fallacious arguments seem very clear examples of rationalization.[10]

The mechanisms of suppression, repression, and rationalization are by no means the only techniques of self-deception. There are a number of others, but there is not sufficient space here to discuss them in detail. The mechanism of *projection* means attributing faults to others in order to conceal one's own guilt from oneself. There is certainly a very common human tendency to blame others for one's own failures. There is also a common tendency to blame some scapegoat group—perhaps "international Jewry"—for social problems instead of accepting the responsibility for attacking these problems personally. *Reaction formation* is the suppression of one's knowledge of a personal fault by developing the opposite virtue in an extreme and bizarre way. One personally troubled by sexual temptations may develop an exaggerated prudery. He convinces himself that one as stern about sex as he is could not possibly have sex problems of his own. *Conversion* or *conversion hysteria* diverts one's attention from troublesome mental content by the development of some physical symptom. The list might be extended, but from what has been said it will be seen that the possibilities of self-deception are extensive and complex.

The mental mechanisms for evading moral issues that have been thus far described operate on the level of the individual. However, group self-deception is also possible. For example, a citizen may have his doubts about the justice of a war, but may refuse to face them, ridding himself of the troublesome ideas by the mechanism of repression. But the country as a whole may do something similar. Public discussion may simply assume without argument that the war is just. The assumption being so universal, it may simply never occur to the individual citizen to question it. One might describe what has happened by saying that the country as a whole has suppressed its guilt feelings so that in the case of the individual the problem does not arise. This sort of thing is probably very common. Such issues as war,

76

slavery, or race relations tend to be exceedingly emotional. Citizens are swept off their feet by waves of passion and in such an atmosphere they do not think calmly and clearly about moral issues. In a sense public propaganda substitutes for private conscience.

The slaughter of some 5,100,000 European Jews under the Nazi government of Germany furnishes a very instructive case study illustrating the various techniques of self-deception, both as practiced by the government itself and by the individuals who obeyed the government's order. The reason why this is such an instructive case study is the fact that after Germany fell, the Allies captured most of the secret archives of all branches of the government. The slaughter of the Jews can therefore be documented in remarkable detail.[11]

The number one technique of the Nazi government was the suppression of facts. As far as possible, information about the destruction process was withheld from all who did not have to participate. There was, therefore, no possibility of open discussion; the public conscience could not be aroused. Among those who knew, all criticism was sternly suppressed. They were not to discuss the subject even among themselves at social gatherings. When it *had* to be discussed, euphemisms were used, such as *Endlösung der Judenfrage* ("final solution of the Jewish question").

The government of the Third Reich rationalized its anti-Semitism in various ways. The people were told that international Jewry was plotting world rule and the destruction of the German people. This being the case, of course the sternest measures against the Jews could be interpreted as justifiable self-defense. Moreover, the Jews were not only conspirators; they were by nature criminal. Indeed, they were actually a lower form of life; they were subhuman. Of course assertions such as these can now be seen by us as the merest nonsense. Yet when they were repeated again and again under the Third Reich in a

77

matter-of-fact style, not only by popular agitators but also by many sober scientists and intellectuals, then it is not altogether surprising that they gradually began to be accepted by the rank and file, perhaps with reservations at first, but then more and more seriously. The appalling fact is that unremitting propaganda can bring about the general acceptance of the most absurd propositions. A whole nation can be morally blinded.

The slaughter of over five million Jews was an enormous undertaking and a very complex one. In one way or another many sections of the government bureaucracy were involved. In some instances this involvement was rather remote. A government accountant might have to keep in order the financial affairs of a death camp; or another official might have to schedule trains to bring to these camps the Jewish victims. Of course, other government officials were involved much more directly. Some were in immediate command of a camp or were leaders of the mobile killing units that followed the army into conquered territories and shot the Jews who were found in captured towns. An important point to remember is that "the bureaucrats who were drawn into the destruction process were not different in their moral makeup from the rest of the population."[12] Even the men in charge of the mobile killing units were ordinary, respectable career men. "These men were in no sense hoodlums, delinquents, common criminals, or sex maniacs. Most of them were intellectuals."[13]

The destruction of the European Jews was of course unspeakably evil. It is hard to imagine a more abominable iniquity. How disturbing it is to realize that the men who engineered this outrage were respected citizens! If such men can carry moral self-deception so egregiously far, what defense is the moral law against social injustice?

It is important to inquire how the men in charge of the destruction process could quiet their consciences and consent to participate in it. After a thorough study of the matter, Hilberg found five rationalizations that they used.[14] One was the doctrine of superior orders. The subordinate's sole duty is to obey. The morality of the orders must be examined by his superior. Second, there was the rationalization that no personal vindictiveness was involved. At the trials of the war criminals most defendants could cite instances of personal favors done by them for individual Jews. To these men it seemed that the absence of personal hatred implied absence of guilt. Third, there was the excuse of remote cooperation. The men who pulled the trigger and shot Jews were indeed guilty of an evil act; but the bureaucrat who merely sat at his desk and signed papers concerned with the destruction process was too remote from the killing to be guiltily involved. Fourth, there was the rationalization that "no man alone can build a bridge." That is to say, the slaughter of the Jews was a vast undertaking involving a vast number of persons, and the contribution of a single individual was so minute that it could be overlooked. Finally, there was what Hilberg calls "the jungle theory." The theory is that it is a law of nature that one must kill to survive. Hitler himself put it into words: "One must not have mercy on people who are determined by fate to perish."[15]

Probably other rationalizations and various other mental mechanisms were employed in addition to those enumerated. The important point is that, whatever mechanisms were used, they proved successful. Men, apparently decent men, participated in inconceivable evil. The fact would not be so horrible if it were unique. But it is not unique. Indeed, as one of the defendants at the Nuremberg trials pointed out, there is a certain parallelism between the slaughter of the non-German Jews by the Nazis and the slaughter of German civilians by the Allies when they bombed noncombatants at Dresden and elsewhere.[16] In either case it was the slaughter of enemy noncombatants. It is rather horrifying to realize that the Americans involved were as successful as their German counterparts in stilling the voice of conscience. In America, as in Germany, convinced Christians simply failed to see how grossly they were violating the New

Testament law of love when they carried out the policies of their government.

It is now possible to give a reasonable explanation for the existence of the Popular Code. Christian doctrine, properly understood, embodies the Authentic Code, the New Testament code of love, as the norm for both private and public morality. However, this code is hard to follow. It often contradicts the mores; and he who deserts the mores for the Authentic Code is apt to find his lot a difficult one. Therefore, both the individual and the community as a whole are apt to take refuge in self-deception and convince themselves that this or that feature of the mores, after all, is not inconsistent with Christian morality. This war *is* just. This form of slavery *is not* a violation of the natural law. And so on. The features of the Authentic Code that are hard to obey are gradually pared away. What is left is the Popular Code, a perverted form of the Authentic Code that does not contradict the mores.

In the meantime the individual Christian enjoys a pleasant sense of moral well-being. He takes an active part in the organized life of his church, liturgical functions, processions, meetings of pious societies. When he thinks of his friends and associates who are not church members, he feels a certain self-satisfaction. They do not guide their conduct by a specific code of religious morality, whereas he himself is proud to identify himself as a follower of Christ.

Catholics go to confession at intervals. A frank examination of conscience, followed by a discussion of one's faults with a trained and experienced confessor, would seem to be an ideal way of unmasking self-deceptions. However, as explained in Chapter II, the examination of conscience is usually based on the Popular Code and this code does not call for a violent break with the mores. As a result, confession is not likely to arouse one's conscience to the type of social evil which has been dis-

80

cussed above. The slaveholders went to confession and continued to hold their slaves.

Of course Christians are not always as blind to the moral aspects of a social issue as they were, for example, in the case of American Negro slavery. Yet even when theologians and publicists point out a social evil, even when actionists demonstrate practical steps toward reform, even when ecclesiastical authority gives its full support, even under these favorable circumstances, reform may not follow. Experience shows that it will not follow unless the conscience of the great mass of believers is aroused. Wise leaders remain ineffective until they attract a sufficiently large body of followers.

In this connection it is instructive to study the history of the Catholic social movement in nineteenth-century Europe. The continued growth of capitalism and the rapid development of the factory system had created problems for the working class. In the absence of government intervention, labor was often outrageously exploited; and the undesirability of such intervention became a dogma of the prevalent "classical" school of economics. In response to these problems an impressive body of Catholic social thought developed which pointed out the existing injustices and demanded control of them by legislation. Among those who helped develop this school of thought were men like Gerbet, Veuillot, Lacordaire, and the Vicomte de Villeneuve-Bargemont in France, Bishop von Ketteler and Canon Moufang in Germany, Cardinal Mermillod in Switzerland, and Cardinal Manning in England. The general principles of the movement received the highest sort of official approbation from the great series of social encyclicals which Pope Leo XIII and his successors published at frequent intervals.[17]

In spite of its impressive character, the Catholic social movement did not attract the loyalty of the working class. Instead, that class became more and more alienated from traditional reli-

81

gion. A number of studies of French Catholics in particular have shown that there is a negative correlation between socio-economic class and religious practice. As one examines the amount of religious observance among those in management, the white-collar employees, the skilled workers, and the unskilled, one finds less and less regularity in each successively lower social class.[18] Although owners and managers tend to be considerably more regular in their religious practices than their employees, it is to be doubted that their faith leads them to accept wholeheartedly all the teachings of the social encyclicals. Léon Harmel in his factory at Val-des-Bois was outstandingly successful in applying practically the principles of social justice to his business, but he had few imitators.

It was the activity of the socialists and later of the communists that won the loyalty of the working class away from the Church. Left-wing social thought developed parallel to that of the Catholic social movement. Count Henri de Saint-Simon is generally considered the father of socialism. In his *Nouveau Christianisme* (1825) he developed a natural religion which was to inspire men to mutual aid through mutual love. The next stage was represented by the utopian socialists—principally Fourier, Owen, and Cabet—who proposed to reform society by setting up small idealistic communities which would demonstrate an ideal economic system and inspire others to follow their example. The February Revolution of 1848 brought Blanc and Proudhon to the fore. The former proposed that capitalism should gradually be abolished and that the state should take over the means of production; the latter emphasized the availability of credit as a factor in social equality. Finally, Karl Marx in his *Das Kapital* developed the full theory of socialist production and distribution. By this time leftist social thought had become thoroughly antireligious and atheistic.

It is important to ask why, as the crisis between capital and labor became more and more acute, the working class turned for guidance to the irreligious socialists and communists, rather than to the proponents of social justice working within the religious framework where the workers traditionally belonged. The loss of the working class by organized religion was a general phenomenon throughout western Europe, but it has perhaps been studied most carefully as it applied to the Catholic Church in France.

Doubtless the essential reason for the failure of the Catholic social movement to attract the working class was the fact that it represented only a minority opinion within the Church. The workers saw too many evidences of the association of Catholicism with conservatism to take this social movement seriously. Under the *ancien régime* the bishops had been closely associated with the court and the nobility; if many of the lower clergy had lived close to the people, it was, after all, the hierarchy that set the tone. The working class was inclined to accept a simplistic interpretation of the Revolution as a victory of good over evil; but the Revolution turned against religion and Catholic writers naturally tended to be critical of it and its effects. After the Revolution the developing bourgeoisie inherited some of the *ancien régime*'s political power and some of its attitudes. Outstanding Catholic leaders, particularly under the Second Empire, often sided with the bourgeoisie in defense of property and vested interests. The same leaders frequently failed to support badly needed social legislation. The clergy, too, were all too often allied to the political right and they were seldom trained realistically to apply the Church's moral doctrine to current social, political, and economic issues.[19] Even when the great social encyclicals of Leo XIII and his successors began to appear, they seemed to the worker tending his machine in a French factory to be too remote and too theoretical to be very relevant.

The French Catholic social movement of the nineteenth century was most admirable in itself, but it never became powerful enough to affect in any important degree the mainstream of the country's social thought. Indeed, it was never realistically accepted by the great mass of French Catholics as the authentic teaching of the Church on the social question. Catholic businessmen and politicians continued to believe what they wanted to believe. They conformed to the current mores and profited by their conformity.

It would be a mistake to write off the French Catholic social movement as a failure. Its contribution was valuable and permanent, as was the case with other Christian reform movements in western Europe. If it had only limited success in its own time and place, it nevertheless accomplished important pioneer work. Without it, our contemporary Christian social movements would be notably poorer.

However badly organized Christianity has failed in reorienting society according to the New Testament ideal, the ideal itself remains infinitely beautiful. One can gain some idea of its beauty by reading the lives of the saints, particularly the lives of the modern saints who lived in our own modern world. The saints took seriously the law of love. They tried earnestly to live by the Authentic Code. Their lives give one some hint of what human society might be like if men made a serious effort humbly to shape their lives by New Testament doctrine.

When one really grasps the meaning of Christ's teaching, it can have a revolutionary effect on his life. I once chanced to talk to a young workingman who had had a conventional parochial-school education, but who had become disillusioned with his religion among the hard realities of working-class life. Then he chanced to read the New Testament and immediately all was changed. He had found something to give meaning to his life. He had found something so important that all else had to be subordinated to it. The miracle had happened in his own life that had happened so often to others; but it was no less miraculous for having often happened.

Society itself has to be awakened to the beauty and to the practicality of the Authentic Code, just as individuals have been so awakened. How can this be brought about? The question is as difficult as it is important. However, in the remainder of this book some suggestions will be offered that may throw light on possible answers.

NOTES TO CHAPTER V

1 For the mind of the Church on freedom of conscience, see Vatican Council II, *Declaration on Religious Freedom.*

2 The concept of mores was developed by William Graham Sumner, a pioneer sociologist at Yale, in his *Folkways, a Study of the Sociological Importance of Usages, Manners, Customs, Mores, and Morals,* originally published in 1906.

3 A full account of the life and death of Jägerstätter is to be found in Gordon C. Zahn, *In Solitary Witness* (New York, Holt, Rinehart and Winston, 1964). There are some further reflections on the subject in the same author's more recent book, *War, Conscience and Dissent* (New York, Hawthorn Books, 1967).

4 Zahn, *War, Conscience and Dissent,* pp. 149-150.

5 The term "parataxis" was used by Thomas V. Moore in his *Dynamic Psychology* (Philadelphia, Lippincott, 1924). The term seems very appropriate, but "mental mechanism" is in more common usage. The mechanisms described in this chapter belong to the subvariety "defense mechanisms" or "parataxes of defense" because they serve as a defense against the consciousness of unpleasant realities.

6 There is a good deal of evidence for the influence of the unconscious on conduct, some of it of a rather technical nature. For example, an experimenter may tell a hypnotized subject to do something after awaking, while forgetting the suggestion given under hypnosis. The subject carries out the order but does not know why. To him, it seems merely a sudden impulse; but clearly it was due to a suggestion that remained on the unconscious level.

7 *Catholic World,* Vol. 161 (1945), p. 499.

8 There are a few hopeful signs which seem to indicate that many

Americans are becoming conscious of the moral questions raised by war. At least in the current discussion of the Vietnam conflict one hears occasional reflections on its rightness or wrongness.

9 Sterling A. Brown, "Negro Character as Seen by White Authors" in Alain Locke and B. J. Stern, eds., *When Peoples Meet* (New York, Hinds, Hayden & Eldredge, 1946), pp. 327-349.

10 Joseph D. Brokhage, *Francis Patrick Kenrick's Opinion on Slavery* (Washington, Catholic University Press, 1955), Chap. 3, develops very well the occurrence of this ambiguity during the slavery controversy.

11 Raul Hilberg, *The Destruction of the European Jews* (Chicago, Quadrangle Books, 1961), is a thorough treatment of the subject.

12 *Ibid.*, p. 649.

13 *Ibid.*, p. 189.

14 *Ibid.*, pp. 658-662.

15 "Man dürfe kein Mitleid mit Leuten haben, denen das Schicksal bestimmt habe, zugrunde zu gehen." Quoted *ibid.*, p. 662.

16 *Trials of War Criminals Before the Nürnberg Military Tribunals,* Vol. 4 (Washington, Government Printing Office, 1949), p. 357.

17 On the general history of Catholic social thought in Europe during the nineteenth century, see Adrien Dansette, *Religious History of Modern France* (2 vols., New York, Herder and Herder, 1961), Michael P. Fogarty, *Christian Democracy in Western Europe, 1820-1953* (Notre Dame, Indiana, University of Notre Dame Press, 1957), Joseph N. Moody (ed.), *Church and Society: Catholic Social and Political Thought and Movements, 1789-1950* (New York, Arts Inc., 1953), and J.-B. Duroselle, *Les Débuts du Catholicisme social en France: 1822-1870* (Paris, Presses Universitaires de France, 1951).

18 Joseph N. Moody, "The Dechristianization of the French Working Class," *Rev. of Politics,* 20 (1958), pp. 46-69. See especially pp. 50-52.

19 *Ibid.*, pp. 53-65.

Part Two

CHAPTER VI

Christian Personalist Action

FACE TO face with a society beset by problems the individual Christian has the obligation of becoming involved. He does not fulfill his complete duty of fraternal charity if he merely succeeds in being right in his relations with his individual neighbors. He also has his obligations as a citizen; and these include that of working actively to overcome social problems and thus create a better society.

Of course all this is alien to the spirit of the Popular Code which demands conformity to the mores but does not demand that one work for the improvement of the mores themselves. The man who lives by this code opens his prayer book and examines his conscience by the list of sins he finds therein. He asks himself whether he has lied or stolen or yielded to bad thoughts. Thus he assesses the state of his soul and he closes the book without asking himself whether he has fulfilled his obligation of interracial love or whether he has dared protest against an immoral war. It has already been pointed out in this book that such an attitude of very limited social responsibility can have very tragic consequences.

There are others with a more sophisticated conscience who do realize that there exists a moral obligation to fight against social injustice. They understand that this can be a very pressing duty for statesmen and other members of the power structure who control the destiny of society. Yet they cannot see that they, too, have a duty. They feel that as private individuals they have no power to act. It is the old rationalization that "no man alone can build a bridge" which, according to Hilberg, was often used by the Nazi bureaucrats to excuse their participation in the slaughter of the European Jews.

As a matter of fact no one has a right to remain passive in the presence of social problems. There is always something that the individual, even the humblest individual, can do.

Even under the most unfavorable circumstances the individual can use the technique of spiritual means to combat social injustice. There is, after all, a type of demon that cannot be exorcised save by prayer and fasting.[1] The lives of the saints provide many striking examples of the power of prayer. These lives, of course, contain many accounts of exploits that cannot stand up under the light of critical history. Yet there remain a great many fully documented examples of the triumphal power of spiritual means. It is a sad mistake to overlook the effectiveness of penance and prayer.

Prayer is more than a means of obtaining visible results. It is an integral part of all social action under the Authentic Code. For this Code demands that human acts be motivated by charity, by love of God and love of man for the sake of God. But love implies an awareness of its object. To direct one's acts toward God, one must be conscious of Him. Thus the volitional life of the Christian must subsist in the presence of God—which is merely a way of saying that it must be a life of prayer. Prayer makes it possible for Christian social action to be God-oriented; and, of course, such orientation is essential.

Every individual, even the most humble, controls the tiny segment of society which consists of his own interpersonal relations, and he can strive to make this tiny segment as perfect as possible. This fact provides him with another technique of social action. If he lives in a rigidly segregated community where Negroes suffer from all sorts of social injustice, it may be that he is powerless to modify the community mores. However, he can strive to be perfect in his own interracial relations. He can uniformly practice love and justice in his social contacts with another race. Or, if he sees the poor oppressed by an unjust economic system, he can probably do little to change the system itself. But he can show his own personal love for the poor by being kind and generous to them. When injustice is rife in the community the individual can accomplish something by refusing to participate in this injustice.

The importance of personal influence, even among the humble and obscure, must not be underestimated. A man who thinks for himself and who expresses his ideas convincingly in discussions with his friends is bound to have a certain effect. The influence of a single individual, viewed in isolation, may be minuscule; but when the thought of many individuals tends in the same direction it can be very important. Public opinion, after all, is thus formed and modified.

It is easy to illustrate the power of public opinion. One interesting example is what happened in Italy when the Fascist government decided to persecute the Jews. The first anti-Jewish measures adopted there were as harsh as any taken in Germany under the Third Reich; but the Italian measures were enforced only half-heartedly. Whatever the government decided, it soon became clear that the people had no enthusiasm for the persecution of the Jews. Public opinion did not approve. Without the backing of public opinion, even a harsh and dictatorial regime like that of Mussolini could do little.[2]

It is clear, then, that one cannot be excused from all social responsibility even under the most unfavorable circumstances. It may be that a totalitarian regime makes organized action for social injustice impossible. Even in a democracy, an individual's lack of ability and resources may prevent him from doing much.

91

However, the fact that a person can contribute only a little to the cause of social justice does not excuse him from the obligation of contributing that little.

The type of social action just described may be appropriately called *personalist* action because it is action truly worthy of a *person*. One may define a person as a being endowed with intellect and free will. He who uses these endowments fully, and only such a one as he, acts as a person in the fullest sense. He tries to base his actions on reason rather than emotion. Therefore, he takes the trouble to gather his facts from the best available sources and he examines these facts impartially. Only thus does he reach a decision. Then he carries out this decision regardless of consequences because this is what right reason requires him to do.[3]

Because the personalist makes his own decisions instead of passively following the crowd, his life is likely to have a strongly marked individuality. This is well illustrated by the lives of the saints. Although they all modeled their lives successfully on the Authentic Code, they were strikingly original in their ways of doing so. They acted rationally in that each interpreted his duty in the light of current social conditions and his own particular state of life. Thus one finds saintly kings and saintly beggars, saintly geniuses and saintly simpletons, saintly hermits and saintly social leaders, saints as different from one another as possible. Personalism begets individuality.

Personalism can be better understood if it is compared with contrasting ways of life. It contrasts sharply, for example, with life in the army. The recruit may be inducted against his will. Afterwards everything possible is done to depersonalize him and rob him of his individuality. His clothes are taken away from him and he is given a uniform. Even his haircut is prescribed. He is despoiled of all personal privacy. Instead of making his own decisions, he is forced to follow orders. Probably he is exposed to propaganda talks and propaganda films; but military leaders are not really very much concerned about what he thinks so long as he faithfully and efficiently carries out orders. Actually the soldier is not treated as a fully human person. He is driven to a course of action desired by the authorities, more or less as a brute beast may be driven.

Totalitarian states are another good example of the antipersonalist way of life. Citizens living under such regimes have neither freedom for discussion nor freedom of choice in civic matters. Thus they lack the two essentials of personalism. They are exposed to a constant barrage of propaganda which appeals to emotion rather than to reason. They are constantly under scrutiny and any deviation from the party line brings prompt retribution. It is a dehumanizing way of life.

Even in a democracy there are often antipersonalist social movements. Characteristically, they represent either the extreme right or the extreme left. People are not likely to join such groups out of reasoned conviction. They join, rather, because the policies of the group are in line with their own prejudices. Thus a violently anti-Negro neurotic may become a member of the Klan because that organization is also violently anti-Negro. Such groups constitute a grave public menace precisely because they are so anti-intellectual. It is unfortunate that human beings make mistakes; yet as long as they are open to reason, there is hope that they can see their errors and correct them. When emotion takes over, this hope is lost. An unreasoning group becomes a mob. When men cease to be rational, they can be incredibly brutal.

Christian social action must necessarily be personalist. It begins with an examination of social conditions in the light of New Testament ideals. This is a rational process. The actionist asks himself what he can do under the circumstances. Then he freely chooses to do it. He does not act under coercion. He does not allow himself to be carried away by emotion. He acts in a fully human way. It is precisely as a human being that he makes the offering of his love.

The foregoing discussion has included examples of action which the Christian personalist may undertake as an individual. However effective such action may be, it is nevertheless normal for the personalist to join with other like-minded persons and to carry out his social action as a member of a group.

Personalist social-action groups have a distinctive character of their own. Usually they begin with a tiny nucleus of thoroughly convinced persons who spend many long hours discussing their principles so that they may be thoroughly understood in all their ramifications. At the same time members begin to apply these principles actively, often in direct and striking ways, for example, by picket lines or civil disobedience. Gradually the group draws attention. It attracts followers. However, there seems to be a rough limit for the size of such a group. It must not become so large that face-to-face discussion is impossible. When the size of the group approaches this limit, it usually splits into small, cooperating groups. When several such groups are formed, one may speak of a personalist social movement.

Personalist action groups contrast with what may be called *mass-action* organizations. The latter are likely to be inaugurated by persons in authority who use their prestige to attract members. The principles of the group are framed by select committees and are imposed from above. Action is likely to follow conventional lines such as lobbying for legislation. The actual management of the organization is usually in the hands of professionals who work in well-managed offices. Interaction among members is seldom of the face-to-face variety. Usually it takes the form of listening to speeches at meetings or reading literature mailed from headquarters. The accomplishments of such mass-action organizations may be excellent, but they tend to be unoriginal. Their spirit is often low-keyed emotionally. Among their members, enthusiasm may be rather restrained.

Personalist groups can be an exceedingly powerful force for social change. In fact, it might be argued that they are the normal means by which such change is brought about. The most striking example of this is the foundation and spread of Christianity itself. Jesus Christ was a very popular leader and attracted a large following; yet He refused to capitalize on this popularity to found a mass movement. "Perceiving that they were about to come to take him and make him king, Jesus withdrew to the mountain, himself alone."[4] If Christianity had been founded suddenly, as a mass movement, if it had been founded by the superficial indoctrination of a great crowd of people, it would have been a superficial movement without roots.

It is instructive to examine carefully what Jesus actually did. He formed a tiny, personalist group of Apostles with whom He was in daily, face-to-face contact. He revealed to them the tenets of His doctrine in a constant daily dialogue. He trained them by precept and by His shining example. It was a group strongly cemented together by Christian love; and by this group experience the Apostles became new men.

At His death, Christ left few followers. There were the Apostles, a more peripheral group of disciples, some personal friends. However, this little group formed a closely knit community whose members "were of one heart and one soul."[5] Those who had more of the world's goods shared with those who had less so that "there was no needy person among them."[6] The earliest Christian community was a fine example of a personalist group. As the Church spread to various cities, the converts formed groups of the same sort. One catches glimpses of them in the Pauline epistles.

Perhaps the most instructive example of the spirit of the early Christian communities is contained in Saint Paul's First Epistle to the Corinthians, precisely because of the criticisms which this epistle contains. The Apostle was surprised and profoundly shocked when he learned that the church at Corinth was disunited. "I hear there are divisions among you and I believe it in part."[7] Saint Paul goes on to say that the union among the members of the Christian community should be like that among the members of the human body; for Christians make up the Mysti-

95

cal Body of Christ. Charity, love, is the greatest of the virtues. It should bind the followers of Christ into an indissoluble unity.

With the passage of centuries, Christianity gradually lost momentum. The early fervor cooled. It is possible to argue that this change took place when the Church slowly changed from a personalist movement to a mass movement. When doctrine was no longer communicated verbally to excited groups of converts but was embalmed in uninteresting books to be taught in the formality of the classroom, it lost something of its fascination. When the bishop ceased to rub shoulders daily with his flock, when he became a remote figure, gorgeously clad, living in a palace, and dealing with his flock through subordinates, then Christianity began to lose its intimacy and to become formal. It began to lose its place as the single, dominating influence in the life of the Christian.

It is a peculiar strength of Christianity that it has within itself an abiding power of self-renewal. Very significantly, the means of this renewal is regularly a personalist movement. When the medieval Church needed an injection of fervor, Saint Francis of Assisi furnished precisely that. His early followers were few, but their spirit was overwhelmingly intense. When abuses within the Church precipitated the Protestant Reformation, Saint Ignatius of Loyola, with a half-dozen followers, took a vow on Montmartre on August 15, 1534, and set in motion what was to be a Counter-Reformation among Catholics. In fact, the early history of nearly all religious communities repeats the same story. The nucleus of the community is a group, very small in numbers, but very intense in its spirit of dedication. The power of groups of that sort has been proved by history again and again. It is a tremendous power.

It is a mistake to look to the hierarchy to initiate renewal. It is not the function of the hierarchy to start social movements, but rather to approve them after they have come into being, to guide them, and to give them status. Rome did not decide to found the Society of Jesus to meet a crying need of the time.

Saint Ignatius and his companions founded it; Rome approved. The Jocistes were not founded by a pope. They began with the small group which the then Father Cardijn gathered around himself in Belgium. What is true in the area of practice is true also in the area of theory. The doctrine of the great social encyclicals of Pope Leo XIII and his successors was not original with them. It originated at the grass-roots level, the product of a long series of original thinkers. What the popes did was to systematize this doctrine and stamp it with their seal of approval.

It has been argued in this book that organized Christianity has scandalously failed to apply New Testament doctrine effectively to the moral problems of society. Religious leaders have not only consented to social evils by their silence; they have often sanctioned these evils and have participated in them. This has been possible because moral doctrine has been compartmentalized. The Authentic Code of New Testament love has been taught in the classroom; it has been meditated upon in monasteries. Yet in practice, when real current problems were being considered, another code has furnished the norm. This code is worldly. It conforms to the mores. It is what is here called the Popular Code.

Obviously reform is needed. A Christian has the strict and solemn duty of guiding his life by New Testament morality; and this duty applies to his relations with society as such, as well as to his relations with his individual neighbors. Until this obligation is widely and realistically accepted by the Christian people, the scandal of Christian social passivity will remain.

The present volume contains no blueprint for reform. It merely insists on a fundamental principle which must be basic in any reform movement, whatever its particular type of organization may be. This is the principle of personal responsibility. The Christian merits heaven when he feeds the hungry, clothes the naked, and practices the other works of mercy. Just how he does these things will depend on circumstances. He may act as an individual or as a member of a group of like-minded persons.

Christian love takes many forms. What is essential, however, is that he accepts the reponsibility of showing his love for his neighbor in some practical way. When, and only when, this spirit of loving service is vastly more widely diffused among Christians than it is at present, will the face of the earth be renewed.

Although this volume contains no blueprint for reform, certain general principles will be considered. These are principles which determine the spirit of Christian social action, not the nature of its formal organization. Christian action can take many forms. It may operate on the level of the individual. It may be embodied in a single face-to-face group or in an enormous international organization containing a multitude of such groups. What, however, must be common to all forms of Christian action is its spirit. It is the spirit of the New Testament, and that admits of no modification. The remainder of this book will discuss the nature of the inevitable spirit of Christian social action.

NOTES TO CHAPTER VI

1 "This kind is not cast out except by prayer and fasting." Mt. 17:20. This clause is missing in some ancient manuscripts and consequently in some modern translations.
2 Raul Hilberg, *The Destruction of the European Jews* (Chicago, Quadrangle Books, 1961), pp. 421-432.
3 What is here described as "personalist" is actually identical with what is "prudent" in the classical theological sense. However, prudence has been so frequently and so grossly misunderstood that if the word were to be used here it might easily cause confusion.
4 Jn. 6:15.
5 Acts 4:32.
6 Acts 4:34.
7 1 Cor. 1:18.

CHAPTER VII

Experience with Personalism

$\mathbf{W}$HAT I have learned about personalist action has been learned by contact with personalist movements. The nature of such action can best be explained if I become autobiographical for a bit and discuss my experience.

In July, 1932, I returned from a year of study in Berlin and Frankfurt. Intellectually, the experience had been most stimulating; but I found the economic and political situation in Germany most depressing. The country was in chaos. Hitler alone had a program which sounded convincing to a majority of the people, and the following spring the tragic decision was made to confer on him dictatorial power.

In 1932 the United States was still deep in the Depression, and conditions were to get worse before they got better. In 1933 the gross national product touched its low point for the period. Deep discouragement was the prevailing mood. However, Franklin D. Roosevelt took office that year and things began to look up.

The Depression had at least one good effect. It made people think. We had long taken the socio-economic system for granted; but now that it was breaking down, we began to examine it critically. For Communists, the Depression was an incontrovertible proof that capitalism was doomed. In the meantime, conservatives counseled patience. Among Catholics, the most convincing voice was that of my friend and colleague, Monsignor John A. Ryan. For over two decades he had been arguing that the doctrine of the great social encyclicals could provide a feasible solution for current economic problems. It seemed to him that the New Deal reflected at least in a general way the spirit of the encyclicals. He accepted the Roosevelt program wholeheartedly, every jot and tittle of it. Most of us agreed with him.

It must have been in the summer of 1934 that Agnes Regan told me about the Catholic Worker house in New York. This remarkable woman, after whom Agnes Regan Hall on the Catholic University campus is named, was at that time Assistant Director of the National Catholic School of Social Service where I used to teach one course. She seemed to be impressed by the Catholic Worker experiment. Since I had great confidence in her judgment, the next time I went to New York I visited the Catholic Worker house, then located on East 15th Street. The experience changed my life.

The thing that overwhelmed me about Dorothy Day, Peter Maurin, and their colleagues was their conviction that the New Testament ought to be taken literally. Christ had warned against the danger of riches, so the Catholic Worker group lived in voluntary poverty. Their house was rundown, shabby, and less than spotlessly clean. Their food and clothing were very plain and simple. Christ had said that it was the Christian's strict duty to give food and drink to the hungry and the thirsty, to clothe the naked, to harbor the harborless; and these were precisely the things the group was doing. Christ preached universal love. We must find Him in all men, even the most humble. It was touching to see the tenderness, utterly unmixed with any trace of condescension, with which the Catholic Worker staff treated the pathetic, broken-down, rejected men and women who came to them for help.

Of course, it should have been perfectly obvious to me that Jesus Christ meant precisely what He said; and it was intensely humiliating to realize that I had not *really* grasped this central fact, not even after four years of theology and a doctorate in sociology. It would perhaps be fair to say, in the terminology of this book, that I had been exposed to the Popular Code in the seminary and at the University, and that the Catholic Worker suddenly brought me face to face with the Authentic Code. I had served for a time as Assistant Director of the Catholic Charities of Washington. We prided ourselves there on our efficiency. We had a genuine concern for the poor. Yet somehow it had never occurred to me that the poor were vastly more than just "cases," that they were our dear personal friends, that we were to love them tenderly and with a certain reverence, seeing Christ in them.

In the years that followed my introduction to the Catholic Worker group I paid many visits to the New York house as well as to branches in other cities. What I remember best about these visits are the discussions we used to have. It seemed to be standard that at a CW house there would be long discussions which seemed to last almost around the clock. People would join the group or drop out, but the talk itself would go on and on.

The discussions covered every possible topic, but they kept returning to one central point of interest, the rethinking of our personal and social philosophies in the light of a literal acceptance of the New Testament. The group's characteristic thought found its way into print principally in the movement's own paper, *The Catholic Worker,* which first appeared in May, 1933, and soon reached a large circulation. Moreover, there were other periodicals edited by persons more or less closely associated with the CW movement and influenced by it. Three of these began to appear in 1936: the *Christian Front,* edited by Norman McKenna and Dick Deverall, the *Social Forum,* published by a group in Canada, and *Liturgy and Sociology,* organ of

101

the Campion Propaganda Committee, an affiliated CW group based in New York.

In the 1930's there was an important intellectual ferment among American Catholics. In the area of social thought the ferment of which I am speaking centered around the CW movement, but innovators in other areas also kept in touch with Dorothy Day and Peter Maurin. For instance, Dom Virgil Michel, founder of the liturgical movement in the United States, maintained close contact until his untimely death in 1938. Everyone was acutely conscious of the liturgy as a social act, and its connection with CW thought and action seemed natural. At the same time, Graham Carey was thinking through a Catholic philosophy of art. His disciple, Ade Bethune, served on the staff of *The Catholic Worker,* which kept carrying her characteristic cuts. Ade could say a great deal with a drawing.

Probably the most important contribution of the CW group to American Catholic social thought was that dealing with war and peace. War seemed to all of us the most horrible antithesis to the Christian ideal of universal love. *The Catholic Worker* became an outlet for anti-war thought. When the nation entered World War II, thought passed over into action. The Association of Catholic Conscientious Objectors was organized under CW auspices and financed by it. This group made it possible for Catholic conscientious objectors to carry out their required Civilian Public Service under Catholic auspices, first at Camp Simon in New Hampshire and later at the Alexian Brothers Hospital in Chicago and at Rosewood State Training School near Baltimore. The group also published a paper, *The Catholic C. O.*

Association with the Catholic Worker group was a very stimulating experience. We felt that Catholic thought was being reinterpreted in a more valid way, a way closer to the spirit of the New Testament. Then, too, we were conscious of being part of a new sort of movement, a personalist movement, which seemed a much better vehicle for social action than the older

Catholic mass movements, which now appeared to us dull and flaccid. The atmosphere of our talks and meetings was exciting. We were shipmates on a common voyage of discovery. It was a pleasantly shared emotional experience.

In the spring of 1935, a group of us at Catholic University who were interested in the CW movement began to meet every Sunday in a vacant classroom. We called ourselves the Campions. Meetings were completely unstructured. We talked about whatever we pleased, usually things relevant to religion and social action. One member of the group was Gladys Sellew who taught at the University. One day at a meeting she announced that she was going to buy a house in a deteriorated section of Washington and live there. This she did in February, 1936. The house faced on Tenth Street, N.W., but behind it, in the interior of the block, was one of the inhabited alleys for which Washington was notorious in those days. The people living there lived in the most dire poverty.

We named the house Il Poverello House. It was appropriate to name it after the Poor Man of Assisi; for it was a dilapidated house without central heating. Moreover, Dr. Sellew tried to conform her life to the poverty of the neighborhood. For a long time she limited herself to fifteen cent's worth of food per day. She helped the alley people in various ways and maintained close friendly contact with them. She also arranged scholarships at Catholic University for some female graduate students, some white, some Negro, who lived with her at Il Poverello House. In 1938, Mary Elizabeth Walsh, who taught sociology at Catholic University, joined the group.

In the 1930's interracial living was sensational in the extreme. As a result the white members of the group were partially cut off from normal social contacts with the white world. The group at Il Poverello House was thus somewhat socially isolated. The result was that they developed very close bonds among themselves. In the early morning they would come to my six o'clock

Mass at the National Shrine. They would see a lot of one another during the rest of the day. They ate, worked, and recreated together. They became a very closely knit group. This very fact was a form of propaganda for interracial justice and charity. The girls at Il Poverello House did not talk much about good Negro-white relations. They exemplified the ideal in their own lives. Of all the things that happened at the house, this interracial living was perhaps the most important.

The Campions in the meantime transferred their meetings to Il Poverello House. One new member was a French citizen, a native of Martinique, named Louis Achille. He had been doing graduate work in English at the University of Paris and he had accepted an offer to teach French for a while at Howard so that he could carry on his study of English in an English-speaking country. He had been active in Catholic social action in France. He was particularly enthusiastic about his association with an organization called *Les Compagnons de Saint-François*.[1] The principal activity of the *Compagnons* was making pilgrimages in the old-fashioned way, on foot, spending the night wherever they could, in barns perhaps or in open fields. A pilgrimage like this was physically taxing and, therefore, a good form of penance. They also used the pilgrimage as a form of propaganda. When they spent the night in a village they would light a bonfire, encourage the villagers to gather round, entertain them with songs, and indoctrinate them with the spirit of Catholic social action.

Louis Achille made me realize more fully something I already knew, that personalist social action was much further advanced in Europe, particularly in France and Belgium, than in this country. In fact, I suspected that the Catholic Worker movement itself derived its spirit, through Peter Maurin, from France. Through Peter and through Louis Achille I had become acquainted with some of the works of writers prominent in the French movement, of whom probably Emmanuel Mounier impressed me most. I had also read a great deal about the Jocistes.

It seemed important for me to visit Europe and see all this at first hand.

On August 15, 1938, I landed at Southampton and spent a week in England, visiting various social-action projects. Two that impressed me greatly were Saint Joseph's House of Hospitality in London and the Catholic Worker house at Wigan, an industrial city in Lancashire, not far from Manchester. These projects were impressive, I say, but they did not seem very novel; for they represented a penetration into England of the spirit of the American CW houses. However, it was interesting to see the familiar CW personalist spirit reacting in an unfamiliar environment.

In Brussels I spent a good deal of time at the headquarters of the *Jeunesse Ouvrière Chrétienne* (Jocistes) and later in Paris I met some of the leaders of the French branch of the movement. The Jocistes are a very class-oriented movement in the sense that they believe a man must find holiness in his own milieu, and, if he is a workingman, he must find it in his working-class milieu. If a truck driver wishes to become a perfect Christian, he need not buy himself a hair shirt. Let him try to practice charity and the other Christian virtues in his daily round of work. Let him bear his daily irritations with patience; they are his hair shirt.

The Jociste slogan, "See, judge, act," is, it seems to me, a very accurate statement of the essence of personalist action. Members of the movement are concerned not only with the general problems of the working class, but more especially with the particular problems of their own city, their own industry, their own factory. They study these problems at length and then try to think of practical steps to solve them.

I was told that if a priest wanted to found a Jociste group, he might select two or three boys from the parish and work with them intensively week after week for an entire year. Only then, when he felt that this tiny nucleus had been thoroughly indoctrinated, would he cautiously begin to add other members. This enormous emphasis on the need to think things through and to act only in the light of the insights thus acquired is, of course, of the very essence of personalism.

While I was in France I naturally wanted to see the *Compagnons* about whom Louis Achille had told me so much. Therefore I looked up one of the leaders in Paris. He told me that the *Compagnons* were having no pilgrimage just then, but that their feminine equivalent, the *Compagnes,* were on pilgrimage, that they were spending the weekend at the little town of Lhuis, not far from Lyons, and that I would be welcome if I wished to visit them there.

I got in Lhuis Saturday night and was lodged in a house in town. The *Compagnes* were lodged less comfortably, mostly in the haylofts of various local barns, I gathered. Abbé Remillieux was there, too. He was to preach at Mass the next day. He was a remarkable man, curé of Notre-Dame-Saint-Alban in Lyons. There he had introduced some startling reforms. For example, he had abolished the different grades of weddings and funerals customary in French parishes. Everyone married or buried at Notre-Dame-Saint-Alban, rich or poor, had the same ceremonies. What was even more sensational, Abbé Remillieux had abolished all collections. He simply had a box in the back of the church where parishioners could drop in their contributions through a slot. At his church there was no "noise of money around the altar."[2]

Sunday was clear and delightfully cool. After Mass, with the sermon by Abbé Remillieux, and after breakfast, the girls gathered at a little open space and sat down on the grass. Then one of them, their leader apparently, got up on her knees, facing the group, and began to talk. I do not remember what she said except that the general topic was the responsibility of a French Catholic girl in the current social situation. What was unforgettable, however, was something unexpressed, yet somehow clearly perceptible. It was the spirit of the group, and that spirit was one of generous dedication to the ideal of Christian love. There was something charismatic about the speaker. Her discourse had an eloquence far beyond her words. The group somehow coalesced into a loving unity and it became powerful. It was somehow revealed to me during those moments what a mighty force Christian love can be. One is often saddened at the ineffectiveness and the indifference of ecclesiastical leadership in the face of social evil; but as long as there remains a spirit such as I see here, I thought, we need not fear that the gates of hell will prevail.

In the summer of 1940, Mary Elizabeth Walsh, who had been living at Il Poverello House, decided to start a house of her own. With two girls who were graduate students at the University, she moved temporarily into an apartment on Florida Avenue while looking for more permanent quarters. This proved more difficult than was expected. Interracial living was still very unorthodox in Washington, and real-estate men were cautious about renting a house to such a group. It was a bit discouraging. One morning the Gospel of the Mass contained the words, *Habete fidem Dei* ("Have faith in God"). So we named the proposed new house Fides House, the house of faith, because we felt that only through faith could we triumph over all the difficulties.

After some months of search, a suitable house was finally located. It was a three-story, six-room house on New Jersey Avenue. The staff moved in early in January, 1941. Although the house fronted on a main thoroughfare, it was close to six inhabited alleys. The people of the neighborhood fell roughly into two social strata, the people who lived on the streets and the people who lived in the alleys. The former usually belonged to the lowest level of steadily employed workers; the latter tended to be more demoralized, to subsist on welfare or on temporary and very unattractive jobs.

The theory behind Fides House was that the staff would live there and simply try to be good neighbors. Living in a squalid

107

neighborhood, they would share at least some of its discomforts, the heat, the noise, the smells, the ever-present rats and vermin, the run-down housing, and thus practice a very real, though not extreme, form of voluntary poverty. At the same time they had some of the skills and resources which could help their neighbors in emergencies. It seemed a practical way to make a contribution to the relief of social problems while holding concurrently a full-time job.

Without any planning in that direction, Fides House began to take on the characteristics of a settlement house. Various people volunteered to carry on activities. Ruthann Brennan started a nursery school. Ruth Harvey ran a sewing club. Seminarians from the Missionary Servants of the Most Holy Trinity came twice a week to run clubs for the boys. Activities continued to increase and we began to boast that Fides House was "the smallest settlement house in the world."

On January 21, 1948, the present Cardinal O'Boyle was installed as Archbishop of Washington. On May 7, we arranged a little reception for him at Fides House. We expected him to stay perhaps half an hour, make a few polite remarks, and be on his way. Instead he stayed and stayed. He talked at length with every member of the staff. He asked innumerable questions. He had, we realized, a social-work background and a very intelligent consciousness of the problems of the inner city. He spoke our language.

In 1949, the Archbishop bought a much larger house around the corner at 219 Eye Street, N.W., and on February 13, 1950, Fides House moved there and began a new program. However, some time passed before certain necessary renovations could be carried through and it was not until May 9, 1951, that the Archbishop blessed the house and full-scale operation began. At Eye Street, Fides House acquired its first full-time employee, Anne Holecko, and experienced office worker who gave up her good job and moved to Fides House to take charge of clerical details.

Emily Milburn, while holding a full-time government job, moved in as Assistant Director, almost another full-time job.

Fides House was now a rather large operation, yet nearly all the work was done by volunteers. Miss Holecko and a part-time cleaning woman were the only paid workers. Many of the volunteers were exceedingly well qualified. There was, for instance, Jewell Gaffney, an experienced nurse who took charge of the health work, and Camille Hayes, an equally experienced social worker, who ran a referral service.[3]

Another distinctive feature of Fides House was the fact that several members of the staff lived there, thus sharing to some extent the life of the neighborhood. In the early days of the settlement-house movement this was a standard feature. The staff members "settled" in the neighborhood. However, this is distinctly less usual in modern settlements. A final, and perhaps the most distinctive, feature of Fides House was its interracial character. In the 1940's, Washington settlement houses were customarily segregated. I remember once visiting one of these located in a solidly Negro neighborhood, but reserved exclusively for whites. I saw a group of little Negro boys standing at the open door and gazing wistfully at the activities within that were denied to them. Since all three Fides Houses were located in Negro neighborhoods, the clientele was almost solidly colored; but the Board of Directors, the resident staff, and the volunteers were interracial from the beginning.

In 1954 the Archbishop moved us again, this time to a large building on the corner of Eight and Q Streets, N.W., which had previously housed a high school. Fides House now became a large operation. A staff of full-time and part-time workers had to be hired. Running the house took a great deal of time. Dr. Walsh and I felt that we could not do justice to our work at the University and to Fides House at the same time. Therefore, in 1958, when we felt that the work was running smoothly at the new location, we resigned. At our suggestion, the house was placed under the care of the Missionary Servants of the Most Holy Trinity who had worked very closely with Fides House from the very beginning and who could certainly be trusted to maintain its characteristic spirit.

Another manifestation of personalist action that impressed me greatly during these years was the Friendship House movement of the Baroness de Hueck. She began in Toronto in 1930, but came to New York City in 1938 and opened a house in Harlem. The movement spread to several other cities. In 1947, the Baroness left New York to found Madonna House in Combermere, Ontario. My contact with the FH movement was principally during the years when the Baroness was actively associated with it in New York.

The Baroness de Hueck has a most unusual background. Born in Nijni-Novgorod, she was educated in Egypt, Paris, Petrograd, and Canada. Among her subsequent experiences was service as a nurse with the White Russian and British forces during the Russian Civil War. This background has given her a great breadth of viewpoint. The Baroness is a woman of great eloquence and a natural leader.

The Harlem Friendship House had a resident staff living in voluntary poverty, plus many volunteers. The group helped their neighbors in their material needs and there was a play center for children. However, the action at FH centered less on the problem of poverty than on the problem of interracial relations. The group taught good race relations by their example, but they also did a good deal of propaganda through the written and spoken word.

I gave a number of retreats and days of recollection for the FH staff. I visited there often and joined the informal discussions which were as usual there as at the Catholic Worker. A good many interesting people were on the staff or came as visitors. There I met Eddie Doherty, a well-known newspaper man, who subsequently married the Baroness. I met young Catholic intellectuals such as Bob Lax or Tom Merton, the future Trappist author. I got well acquainted with many members of the staff. My association with Friendship House was most pleasant as well as spiritually profitable to me.

During these years I had contact with a number of social-action projects in addition to those enumerated. I must mention two of these. One was the work carried on at Saint Francis Xavier University, Antigonish, Nova Scotia. The University had an extension department which was active in promoting self-help projects, such as credit unions and cooperative stores throughout the province. The level of living in many districts was low. The people were encouraged to help themselves, first by studying their local problems in study clubs and then by taking whatever measures were feasible to solve these problems. At Reserve Mines, I was able to visit Father James J. Tompkins, who played a very large part in the genesis of the movement.

In the summer of 1948, a group consisting largely of persons somehow associated with Fides House went to Europe with me and visited various action projects. What interested us most on this trip was the priest-worker (*prêtre-ouvrier*) movement. This was an effort to lead the working class back to the Church. Unfortunately the Church had become identified with the middle class and the well-to-do in the minds of the workers. Of course the Communists were happy to capitalize on this sentiment and stir up anticlericalism. Therefore a few priests received permission to live as workmen. They worked in factories or on construction sites or on docks, wearing the usual clothes of laborers, and living by twos or threes in working-class districts. They enjoyed certain unusual permissions. For example, they were allowed to celebrate Mass partly in French after work at home in the evening. Our group attended a couple of these Masses. In those days a vernacular Mass in the afternoon was a startling innovation. The priest-worker movement extended over the years 1944 to 1954, at which latter date it was suppressed by Rome.[4]

111

The movement was always small; there were never over a hundred priest-workers. We were intensely interested in the movement because it illustrated how unconventional a daring form of Catholic social action may be.

What I saw at the various action projects described above gave me much food for thought.[5] The most important lesson of all was certainly the importance of taking the Authentic Code, the New Testament law of love, as the supreme norm for human society. All the projects had a certain greatness because they earnestly tried to take this principle seriously. One might quarrel with the concrete application of the principle by this or that movement. One might dispute their judgment on the rightness or wrongness of a specific social situation. But their devotion to fundamental Christian principles was magnificent!

The actionists accepted the Authentic Code in theory; but they also made sincere efforts to put it into practice in their own lives. This is not to say that they had no faults. There were, alas, occasional scandals among them. Then there was often a neurotic fringe of those who would join a movement not out of rational conviction, but in an unconscious and irrational attempt to solve some hidden personal problem. Then there is the common temptation of the actionist to feel smug and superior. An amusing example of this was a little group I met in Paris who blandly used to refer to themselves as "the Christians" (*les chrétiens*) while everyone else in the Church was lumped together and referred to sarcastically as "the right thinkers" (*les bien pensants*).

Yes, they had their faults. Yet, taken all in all, the persons I met at these various action projects were the most impressive group of Christians it has ever been my privilege to meet. Over the years I came to know many of them intimately. I knew some who for years had led thoughtless, self-indulgent lives, but who, through contact with some personalist project, had been transformed. The lives of many of these boys and girls had a transcendent inner beauty. This beauty was incomparable because nothing in the universe is as beautiful as holiness.

The facts of the last paragraph reinforce a truth of paramount importance. Virtue is social. It is not enough to love our family, our friends, our acquaintances. Christian love comes into existence only when one begins to love enemies and outcasts, persons in whom one finds no natural attractiveness. I saw enough of this sort of love at the Catholic Worker, at Il Poverello House, at Fides House, at Friendship House, and elsewhere to leave me breathless. Nothing so beautiful has ever touched my life.

NOTES TO CHAPTER VII

1 The spirit of the movement is well documented in Joseph Folliet, *La Spiritualité de la route* (Paris, Bloud & Gay, 1936).

2 "Bruit d'argent autour de l'autel." On this, see Abbé Michonneau, *Paroisse, communauté missionaire* (Paris, Éditions du Cerf, 1945), pp. 301-332.

3 Mrs. Hayes later held the position of Consultant at the D.C. Department of Public Welfare. Her chief accomplishment there was to establish a very successful and unique center for the training of mothers receiving Aid to Families with Dependent Children to enable them to become self-supporting. After the untimely death of Mrs. Hayes, the name of the institution was changed to The Camille B. Hayes Training Center.

4 Recently Pope Paul VI agreed to give the priest-workers another chance. It is said that there are now forty-eight of them.

5 Some of this is digested in three books I wrote during the period: *Fire on the Earth* (New York, Macmillan, 1936), *Three Theories of Society* (New York, Macmillan, 1937), and *The Mystery of Iniquity* (Milwaukee, Bruce, 1944).

CHAPTER VIII

Be Ye Separate

THE CHRISTIAN living in a wordly society can cooperate as long as the mores do not contradict his principles. He can cooperate, for example, in programs for crime control or for the improvement of public health. However, it is practically inevitable in such a society that sooner or later he will be asked to follow certain mores which contradict his code of Christian love. When this happens, his duty is clear. He must proudly refuse his cooperation. He must follow Saint Paul's mandate to the Corinthians: "Come out from among them, and be ye separate."[1] To understand what this duty means in the concrete, it will be helpful to return to an instance that has already been cited.

When twelve American bishops gathered on May 17, 1840, for the Fourth Provincial Council of Baltimore, no problem more deeply disturbed the American conscience than the problem of slavery. At the time of the Revolution there had been a good bit of antislavery sentiment, even in the South. But then Eli Whitney invented the cotton gin, the raising of cotton on plantations became very profitable, and more and more slaves were needed for these plantations. Southerners closed ranks in staunch defense of slavery. In the meantime an extremely militant Abolitionist movement arose in the North and grew rapdily in strength during the 1830's. By the time the bishops met that day in Baltimore, the controversy had become very vehement. Since this was fundamentally a moral controversy, it seemed logical to expect some pronouncement on it from the bishops.

The slavery issue was brought before the Council dramatically when Pope Gregory XVI's Constitution *In supremo apostolatus fastigio,* dealing with the slave trade, was read there. It had been issued the previous December. In this document the Holy Father instanced a number of earlier condemnations of the trade by his predecessors. Then he went on to say: "We therefore wish to banish from Christian lands such an infamy as this. . . . By our Apostolic authority We admonish all Christians of whatever condition and strongly implore them in the Lord never in the future to dare to harass or despoil of his goods or to enslave anyone, or to give help and encouragement to others doing these things, or to engage in that inhuman commerce by which Negroes . . are bought and sold and in the meantime subjected to most harsh labor."[2]

The particular aspect of slavery on which the Holy Father had concentrated his attention, namely, the slave trade, was itself a hot issue in 1840. It is true that in 1808 Congress had exercised the power granted it by the Constitution and had abolished the legal slave trade. However, the great demand for slaves on the cotton plantations made smuggling very profitable indeed. This was, of course, illegal; but federal officials were cautious in enforcing the law for fear of offending the powerful Congressional delegations from the slave states. In addition to the international slave trade, there was a flourishing domestic one. The use of slaves in the tobacco regions of the Upper South declined just when the demand for them rose in the Cotton Belt. It thus became profitable to sell slaves from the former region to the latter. By 1840 the slave trade was big business in the United States.

The bishops had a good deal to say on a number of moral issues before the Council adjourned. They condemned secret societies; Catholics who joined them were to be refused the sacraments. Those labor unions which also had an air of secrecy were deprecated, particularly since excessive drinking was common at their meetings. Priests were to warn the faithful against the grave evils of mixed marriages. Temperance societies were praised. Sunday was to be kept holy; Catholics should be particularly careful on that day to avoid places where intoxicants are sold. Dangers to the faith of Catholic pupils in public schools were discussed. The bishops seemed resolved to uphold a high and strict code of Christian morality. Yet they passed over in silence the overwhelming moral issue of slavery. They had not a word of support for the Holy Father's condemnation of the slave trade.[3]

It is rather difficult now a century and a quarter later to understand the Council's complete failure to respond to the Pope's pronouncement on slavery. To say that he was condemning only the African slave trade and not the domestic trade in the United States seems a bit disingenuous.[4] His condemnation of "that inhuman commerce by which Negroes . . . are bought and sold" was not modified by any restriction as to locality. Moreover, one would have had to be extremely naïve to remain unaware of the flourishing illegal slave trade between Africa and the United States. It has been estimated that between 1808 and 1860 at least 250,000 slaves were thus imported.[5]

Possibly the most plausible explanation of the bishops' silence was their desire not to stir up further anti-Catholic sentiment at the time. The 1830's had been a decade of increasingly virulent propaganda against the Church. There were exposés of alleged plots for the enslavement or mass murder of American Protestants by hordes of Catholic immigrants. In 1836, the *Awful Disclosures* of Maria Monk appeared, with fanciful stories of debauchery, murder, rape, and infanticide in a convent, all described in profuse detail. Nor was hostility confined to words.

116

The burning of the Ursuline Convent at Charlestown, Massachusetts, on August 11, 1834, became a symbol of the violence with which Catholics were threatened.

Under the circumstances a strong condemnation of the slave trade or of slavery in general might have been politically disastrous. It would have infuriated the enemies of the Church in the slave states and would have given them just the sort of ammunition they needed. On the other hand it would not have helped the Church greatly in the North where the Abolitionists, though extremely vocal, were still not very powerful. The climate of opinion being what it was, the bishops apparently decided to remain silent on the slave trade in order to avoid the unpleasant consequences of an endorsement of the papal position.

The dilemma of the bishops in 1840 is a common one. It is a dilemma faced not only by national hierarchies, but by lay organizations, by editors and publicists, and indeed by individual Christians. The general principle is clear; the believer must not cooperate with a worldly civilization by following its immoral mores. He must come out from among them and be separate. There can be no doubt about this duty. What is less evident is the exact form the duty takes in specific instances. The matter calls for some discussion.

First of all, it is surely evident that the Christian must always profess the principles of his moral doctrine. He must let it be known in public that he adheres to the Authentic Code. This is merely a specific instance of his duty to profess his faith. A great many martyrs have died because they refused to deny the faith by some merely symbolic act, such as stepping on a cross or throwing a pinch of incense on a fire burning before the statue of some heathen god. But is it not, in a very real sense, also a denial of the faith to support as right that which the New Testament condemns as evil?

Of course, it must be admitted that in the complex world of human events it is not always immediately evident which policy

117

is morally right and which is morally wrong. It is easily understandable, for example, how individual Christians may find it hard to decide with moral certainty whether a particular war is just or unjust. However, there are some clear certainties. For instance, there cannot be the slightest doubt that war, like all other human activities, is subject to the principles of morality; no Christian can deny that. It is also hard to understand how any sincere person could doubt for an instant that Pope Gregory XVI was simply applying elementary Christian social doctrine when he condemned the slave trade.

If it is the Christian's duty to condemn social evil, it is still more emphatically his duty not to participate in it personally. Obviously, he must not be a direct and immediate cause of the evil. He must not be the man who pulls the trigger or drops the bomb. But his duty extends far beyond this. In a complex society, what a person does may have distant effects that are not immediately obvious. A Nazi bureaucrat, sitting at his desk and signing papers, might thus play his part in the operation of a death camp hundreds of miles away. Such a man would have to share the guilt for the slaughter of the Jews though he never even saw a death camp, for without the support of the bureaucracy, the slaughter would not have been possible. One can sin simply by being a member of a team.

In addition to the Christian's duty of repudiating social evil and his duty of refusing to participate in it, there is a third duty, that of trying to lessen the evil by positive action against it. As was said in an earlier chapter, no Christian can avoid this duty. He must always engage in personalist action, at least privately, as by prayer. Sometimes, however, his duty extends beyond this and he must join in public social-action movements. This latter obligation, however, is a conditional one; for such action is not always possible. No one can blame the early Christians because they did not agitate for the abolition of slavery by mass meetings and protest marches. Any such action would have been suppressed immediately and would have been perfectly futile.

Similarly there is no ground for criticism when one finds no organized Christian social action under a Communist regime. However, it is harder to excuse passivity in a democracy. In the movement leading to the abolition of slavery in the United States, the churches played parts of varying importance; yet it is probably true that the chief impetus behind the movement came from secular European egalitarian thought rather than from the application of Christian principles. For many of us, this is not a comforting thought.

To summarize—the duty of separating oneself from the mores of a worldly society, the duty of *nonparticipation,* as it may be called, rests on three bases. First, by condemning the evil mores, the Christian separates himself from others intellectually. He proclaims his faith in a different code of social conduct, the Authentic Code of the New Testament. Secondly, he separates himself also by his conduct when he refuses to participate in the observance of those mores he condemns. Finally, he does what he can to abolish the evils in which he refuses to participate. It is thus clear that the Christian in a worldly society, if he takes his religion seriously, is a man apart.

The preceding principles concerning nonparticipation make frightful demands on the Christian actionist. If he takes them seriously, he becomes a pariah. If the bishops in 1840 had condemned slavery, or even if they had condemned only the slave trade, they would, as already remarked, have stirred up a tempest of anti-Catholic hatred. If the German bishops had merely preserved a sullen silence during Hitler's war, instead of actively supporting it, the result would probably have been discrimination against German Catholics and great hardship for them. If American Catholics had taken a stand against all bombing of noncombatants in World War II and had refused to participate in it, they would doubtless have suffered unpleasant consequences.

Many serious Catholic writers have argued that it would be

119

wholly unrealistic to expect believers to practice nonparticipation to the extent implied by the examples of the last paragraph. Thus Guilday, the historian of the Councils of Baltimore, writes in connection with the 1852 Council: "Perhaps the outstanding proof of the wisdom of our prelates lies in their silence over the slavery question. . . . Many expected at the time that this largest and greatest of all Catholic official assemblies in our history up to 1852 would take cognizance of the Church's position; but the hierarchy rejected the apparent demand for such a decision."[6]

Clearly, then, there exists an alternative to the theory of nonparticipation propounded above. This is the alternative chosen by the bishops and praised by Guilday. It consists in a systematic effort to keep lines of communication open between the Church and a worldly society. The world must not be antagonized. By being consistently inoffensive and cooperative, the Church gradually earns the world's good will. Then fruitful dialogue can ensue. Finally, perhaps, this will lead to the conversion of some worldly people and ultimately the Church grows in strength.

This alternative strategy puts great emphasis on the maintenance of peace and calm. For Guilday, this was a sufficient reason to justify the bishops' silence. "When, therefore, as the Council proceeded, it became evident that the attending prelates had decided to keep silent on the question, neither condemning nor condoning slavery, Catholics realized more acutely than ever the real meaning of the Church's place in American life, and non-Catholics appreciated the fact that here was a body of American spiritual leaders who meant to bring to the disturbed condition of the times, the one asset the country needed: peace and calm."[7]

During much of the country's history, the Catholic minority has had a high proportion of immigrants. This fact, plus the fact that Catholics owe ecclesiastical allegiance to a foreign Pope, has given the Church an un-American quality in the view of many people. Anti-Catholic nativism has had a long history here. Naturally, Catholics have been anxious to overcome these prejudices against them. They have tried to demonstrate their patriotism by repeated assertions of loyalty, often in very exaggerated language. Their desire to be accepted has sometimes seemed downright pathetic. It is in this spirit that church leaders have so often refrained from criticism of social evils in order to placate their fellow Americans.[8]

There have just been discussed two divergent ways by which a Christian may react to social evil. One is the technique of nonparticipation. This means that he will publicly disapprove the social evil, that he will refuse to be a party to it by his actions, and that he will do what he can to bring it to an end. The alternative technique is conciliation. Instead of attacking the evil directly, the Christian tries to conciliate those who practice it, to win their good will, to establish dialogue with them, and thus perhaps be in a position ultimately to persuade them to reform.

In choosing between the two techniques, one faces the inescapable fact that conciliation can yield many pleasant consequences. If the Catholic Church in the United States had not proved so conciliatory under a series of great national leaders— England, Hughes, Ireland, Gibbons, Spellman, and others—it could never have attained its present greatness. It could not have become a ten-billion-dollar operation. There could not have been a Catholic President. There would have been more prejudice, discrimination, perhaps active persecution. At first glance the evidence seems overwhelming. Conciliation is the policy of choice. Conciliation as a strategy, however, has one overwhelming disadvantage. It makes impossible the construction of a new society according to the guidelines of Jesus Christ, for, in order to change the current society, one must be free to criticize it. One must be free to point out where present mores conflict with New Testament ideals. If one keeps silent in order to conciliate the worldly, this, of course, cannot be done.

Jesus Christ did not follow the policy of conciliation. His was the very difficult task of introducing new and revolutionary religious ideals. One might have thought that He would begin by trying to conciliate the contemporary religious leaders, the Pharisees. By praising what was good in their doctrine and passing over what was not good, He might have secured their good will. At least He might have tempered their opposition. Again, since Jesus was poor and lacked the prestige of riches, would it not have been prudent for Him to make some rich friends and through them gain access to community leaders? With the backing of a few powerful allies, could He not have made a more successful popular appeal?

Jesus Christ did not try to conciliate the Pharisees and the wealthy. On the contrary, He denounced their sins in strong, clear, direct language. He did this at a frightful cost to Himself, for He earned their unflagging hatred. They harassed Him, persecuted Him in every way. Finally they compassed His death.

He who wishes to be a follower of Jesus Christ must be prepared to do what He did. He must be prepared to proclaim the Gospel, including all the social implications of the Gospel. If he foresees that persecution will result, this is no excuse for inaction. To buy "peace and calm" by a studied silence on such an overwhelming moral evil as American Negro slavery is not a truly Christian policy. Speaking out may call for heroism, for the acceptance of suffering; but the New Testament does not promise the Christian an untroubled life. "They will deliver you up to tribulation and put you to death; and you will be hated by all nations for my name's sake."[9]

Nonparticipation can be a very effective technique of social action. By separating oneself and adopting a special way of living, one dramatizes one's rejection of the current mores. This is a technique particularly suited for individuals and small action groups. It is less well suited for large mass organizations; for nonparticipation tends to be unconventional and daring and it is hard to get the necessary consensus in a large group. The propaganda value of nonparticipation may be illustrated by some examples.

When Dorothy Day and the members of the Catholic Worker staff insist on living in the slums, eating very plain food, and wearing second-hand, donated clothing, they separate themselves sharply from a world that puts a very high value on material success. It is almost everyone's ambition to live in an exclusive neighborhood, own a good car, and dress in the latest fashion. When the CW group rejects these ideals so decisively, then their viewpoint becomes very clear.

When the girls at Il Poverello House and Fides House lived interracially in the segregated Washington of thirty years ago, they too made themselves conspicuous. It was very clear, even to the most casual observer, that they rejected the local mores which decreed the separation of the races.

When David Miller, Tom Cornell, and others burned their draft cards in public, no one could possibly miss the point. They set themselves apart from the mass of American youth who, willingly or not, followed the draft regulations.

The nonparticipation of the Christian actionist is not always well received by his fellows or his superiors. They may be following a conciliatory policy and they are embarrassed by the very contrary policy of the actionist. On October 27, 1967, Father Philip Berrigan, S.S.J., and three others, including a United Church of Christ minister, walked into the Selective Service office in the Baltimore Customs House. They asked to see their own records. When shown the file cabinets, they opened their brief cases, took out small bottles of blood, and poured them over the records. They stated that the blood was their own and that they had poured it over the files to call attention to "the pitiful waste of American and Vietnamese blood 10,000 miles away." They were, of course, arrested. The Baltimore Archdiocesan Chancery Office issued a statement deploring the demonstration and calling it "disorderly, aggressive and extreme."

It was a busy day in the Temple at Jerusalem, for the

123

Passover was at hand. In the Court of the Gentiles the money-changers were busy changing foreign coins, which the pilgrims had brought with them, into local currency. Others were selling oxen, sheep, and pigeons to those who wished to offer them in sacrifice. Then suddenly an Angry Man strode in. He over-turned the tables of the money-changers and the coins rolled across the pavement in hopeless confusion. Then, whip in hand, He drove them all out, along with the oxen and the sheep. All was noise and confusion. The bleating of the sheep mingled with the indignant protests of the merchants. It was an unprece-dented scene. Jesus Christ did not attack abuse with mild, per-suasive criticism. He acted directly, violently.

Would the Baltimore Archdiocesan Chancery Office deplore all this as "disorderly, aggressive and extreme"?

NOTES TO CHAPTER VIII

1 2 Cor. 6:17. St. Paul is quoting the thought of Is. 52:17, but with some change of wording.
2 Henricus Denzinger and Adolfus Schönmetzer, *Enchiridion Symbolorum,* 32nd ed. (Friburg, Herder, 1963), Nos. 2745-2746.
3 Peter Guilday, *A History of the Councils of Baltimore* (New York, Macmillan, 1932), pp. 120-129.
4 This was Bishop England's position. See Madeleine Hooke Rice, *American Catholic Opinion in the Slavery Controversy* (New York, Columbia University Press, 1944), pp. 66-70.
5 For a good brief summary and further references, see "Slave Trade, The American" and "Smuggling of Slaves" in *Dictionary of American History* (New York, Scribner, 1940).
6 Guilday, *op. cit.,* p. 182.
7. *Ibid.,* pp. 169-171.
8 Dorothy Dohen, *Nationalism and American Catholicism* (New York, Sheed and Ward, 1967), gives an excellent account.
9 Mt. 24:9.

CHAPTER IX

Bearing Witness

IN THE New Testament the preaching of the Gospel is often described by the Greek word *martyreo* ("I bear witness") and its cognates. The word is most appropriate. A man may be a bit careless and inaccurate in his everyday conversations; but if he is brought into court, put under oath, and placed on the witness stand, then he realizes that he must tell only that which he knows to be true. Important decisions may rest on his testimony; so he will be very serious about it. He who preaches the gospel is like the witness in court. He dare not speak lightly. He must weigh his words. Then he must speak with conviction.

The mission of John the Baptist is thus described: "He came for testimony, to bear witness to the light that all might believe through him."[1] Note that the purpose of John's testimony was to carry conviction. Because his preaching had the special quality of "bearing witness," it moved the hearers to belief.

Jesus Christ Himself described His teaching in the same language. To Nicodemus, He stated, "We bear witness to what we have seen."[2] In a discussion with the Pharisees, He declared, "I bear witness to myself, and the Father who sent me bears witness to me."[3] The most solemn proofs of the truth of Christ's mission are thus described in terms of bearing witness. He bore witness to Himself by His works and words, and the Father bore witness to Him in Scripture, and by the voice from heaven.

The Apostles were to continue the teaching mission of Christ. Therefore, it is not surprising that their preaching, like His, should be described as bearing witness. During the solemn moments before the Ascension, He charged them: "You shall be my witnesses in Jerusalem and in all Judea and Samaria and to the end of the earth."[4] The Apostles themselves described their own work in similar language. Peter, for example, in his discourse after the descent of the Holy Spirit, affirmed the truth of the Resurrection with the words, "This Jesus God raised up, and we are all witnesses of it."[5] In his discourse to Cornelius he used the same expression. "We are witnesses to all that he did both in the country of the Jews and in Jerusalem."[6] Paul used a cognate term in explaining his mission before Agrippa. "I stand here testifying both to small and great."[7]

The Apostles spoke with the assurance of witnesses because they spoke of what they had seen and heard personally or of what they had other but equally convincing grounds for accepting. The Christian social actionist must be assured that his application of gospel truth to particular social conditions rests on a sound basis. He must study and think through what he is to say before he says it.

In order that the Christian actionist may speak with conviction, two conditions must be met. First, he must have an accurate knowledge of current social facts. Otherwise he will simply miss the point. Secondly, he must have a very deep appreciation of New Testament morality as it applies to society. Otherwise his social criticism will not be genuinely Christian. If he is to bear witness, as the term is used here, he must be deeply grounded in both areas of knowledge.

Before any intelligent social action can be planned, it is necessary to have some insight into cause and effect as they exist in human society; for intelligent diagnosis is impossible without some knowledge of causes; and treatment is impossible unless one knows how to bring about a certain desired effect. All this, however, is difficult. The motives of any single human individual and their effects on his behavior are hard to understand with any completeness. The difficulty is multiplied when one tries to comprehend the interaction of several of these complex human beings. It is hardest of all to understand social interaction if it takes place in a socio-economic stratum very different from one's own.

During the last four summers preceding the present writing, riots have occurred in the Negro ghettos of over a hundred American cities. This rioting has called forth all sorts of comment. There has been much talk of a Communist conspiracy. There have been frequent mentions of police brutality as a cause. There have been smug reflections on the breakdown of law and order. However, as time went on, reflective men began to realize that none of these simplex explanations could be accepted; for behind the rioting lay an extremely complex reality, a ghetto mentality, a ghetto culture, which is very hard for anyone to comprehend, especially one belonging to the white-collar class.

Of course some facts about ghetto life are easy to obtain. One can get death rates, infant-mortality rates, statistics about unemployment, deteriorated housing, crime, and delinquency. One can compare these figures for the ghetto and for white-collar areas and thus get a clear statistical picture of human misery. One can walk through the slums and see the overcrowding, the lack of play space, the shabby schools, the broken glass and filth scattered about. One can smell the stench of the slums. Yet all this, impressive as it is, does not explain the riots. To explain the anger of the ghetto dwellers, one must know what it feels like to be one. Behavioral scientists have coined the word *empathy*, literally "a feeling into." It means putting oneself imaginatively into another's place and seeing the world through his eyes. To

127

understand the riots, and the problems of the ghetto in general, one needs empathetic understanding.

To understand the ghetto mentality, one must try to imagine first of all what it is like to grow up educationally deprived. Even during infancy the intellectual development of the slum child is handicapped by the culturally deprived atmosphere of his home, the lack of a delicately expressed maternal love, the absence of toys for him to manipulate, the scarcity of language directed to him.[8] The public school he attends is likely to be one of the poorer ones of the city's school system. The curriculum fails to hold his interest. He drops out almost automatically as soon as he reaches the minimum age at which this is permissible. Then, as a teen-ager, he looks for a job. But he is a Negro and a school dropout with no special vocational skills and he finds it impossible to find really satisfactory employment in the present automated and technologically complex economy.[9] He may try to subsist on a series of temporary jobs or he may find employment in some such occupation as dishwasher that offers no opportunity at all for advancement. He sees stretching before him a life of abject poverty.

Almost every aspect of ghetto life has its distinctive quality which sets if off from middle-class life. An illiterate woman living in the slums may not dare to wander more than two or three blocks from her home; she cannot read the street signs and she would be lost if she wandered farther. Slum people speak their own dialect of English with its own vocabulary, its own phonetics, its own inflections, and its own syntax.[10] It is a dialect quite distinct from the standard English of the white-collar people. Thus language forms an additional barrier between the two groups. Family life is different in the ghetto. There is more illegitimacy and more common-law marriage; more homes are headed by a woman. In the ghetto there is more violent crime. What was said in an earlier chapter about white-collar crime should make it clear that those who live in the inner city are not necessarily less law-abiding than those in suburbia; but the typical crimes of the two areas are very, very different.

It would be easy to multiply contrasts between life in the ghetto and life elsewhere, but space is lacking. However, it is important to point out that these multiple differences have an overwhelming psychological effect. They produce a feeling of alienation. One's emphatic understanding must include this feature or it will be very limited. The word "ghetto" is really very appropriate. The slums are surrounded by no wall; but the poor are confined there in a very real sense. They are confined there physically because they do not have the income to move out. Yet what is even more serious is the psychological barrier which cuts off these Negro ghetto-dwellers from any genuine participation in the social and economic life of the community. This isolation is very cruel. No one can go before the general community to bear witness about life in the ghetto unless he grasps this central fact.

Empathy is needed to understand any social situation. It is needed to understand the inner-city Negro ghetto which has been used here as an example; but it is equally needed to understand the situation of the poor whites of Appalachia, of the Mexican-American agricultural workers in the Southwest, of the Puerto Ricans in New York City, or of the starving rural Negroes in Mississippi. Statistics and the observation of the visible facts yield only a superficial view.

If empathy is so important, then it is important to ask how it is to be acquired. How, for example, does one gain an empathetic knowledge about the social realities of an inner-city slum? It is acquired through close interhuman relations with the people of that area. One must not remain an outsider. One must spend time among the area people, sympathizing with them in their grief, helping them in their misfortunes, sharing their joys as well as their sorrows, until acquaintances ripen into friend-

129

ships and a mutual trust is established. Gradually people begin to talk freely. They begin to discuss facts not ordinarily admitted to outsiders. Such are the foundations of empathy.

It is important to realize that inner-city people have their reticences. They tend to feel defensive toward the people who come into the neighborhood from the alien white-collar world. One rather natural defense is to tell these people what it is thought they would like to hear. The social worker is told what may be expected to make a favorable impression, so that one may perhaps be retained on the relief rolls. An eager graduate student, notebook in hand, comes and asks leading questions; it is not surprising that the answers he gets confirm his hypothesis. The moral of all this is that superficial contacts yield deceptive results.

It is a helpful strategy to take up residence in the neighborhood in which one is interested and to adopt for oneself something approximating the level of living prevalent there. The Catholic Worker and Friendship House centers in various cities and Il Poverello House and Fides House in Washington, for example, all had resident staffs of people who had moved from their native white-collar districts to the inner-city neighborhoods where these centers were located. To be willing to share slum life creates confidence. A readiness to make this sacrifice proves that one's interest in the neighborhood is genuine. It is important to note, however, that no white-collar person can *really* become part of a slum neighborhood. He may accept all the material disadvantages of the area level of living as far as food, clothing, shelter, recreation, even health care, are concerned. Yet he knows that he has the skills and the background to resume his middle-class way of life, should he care to do so. He can never share the despair of the slum dweller who knows that he must forever stay where he is and that there is no hope of escape.

The Christian actionist is acutely conscious of the importance of the empathetic knowledge which he has developed personally, but this should not cause him to overlook the value of contributions made by various scientific disciplines. Thus medical men can interpret the health problems of the area with the sources of disease and the needed remedies. Psychiatrists can assess the effect on mental health of the abnormal living conditions of the slums. Educators and educational psychologists can give sophisticated explanations of the poor school performance of inner-city children. Experts on city planning can suggest feasible schemes for the physical rehabilitation of slum neighborhoods. Other specialists have other particular contributions to make. However, if the suggestions of the experts are to be applied not mechanically but in a human and humane manner, then they must be applied by those who understand the area people and the area mentality. There is, after all, no substitute for empathetic insight when a program of reform is to be worked out and applied.

If it is important for the Christian actionist to gain insight into social situations, it is far more important for him to be able to apply his moral principles to them. To do this, it might seem logical to turn to treatises on social justice written by moral theologians; for it is their task to reduce Christian morality to concrete terms and apply it practically to society. Such writers, however, are apt to be concerned with the definition and delimitation of sins against social justice, rather than with a description of the Christian ideal. They often give the impression that they are more concerned with the minimum standard that must be met if one is to save one's soul than with the maximum standard, the inspiring social ideal toward which Christians are called to strive.

The concrete application to specific situations of the Christian ideal, the law of love, should be sought through prayer and contemplation. The human mind ordinarily arrives at new truths by the process of discursive reasoning, progressing laboriously from known premises to new conclusions. Yet the mind can sometimes immediately apprehend a new truth; it sees the truth straightway and without discussion. Perhaps the most appro-

131

priate name for this process is *noësis*.[11] A simple example would
be an analytic judgment such as, "The whole is greater than any
of its parts." However, noësis can go far beyond such simple
judgments. When one listens to a Beethoven symphony or
watches the play of sunshine on an Italian lake, when one reads
of heroic deeds or reflects on the beauty of love, one appre-
hends inexpressible realities, truths that lie too deep for words.
It is the same with religious contemplation. When one asks what
is the Christian thing to do, the loving thing, in a specific social
situation, one often cannot find the answer by dry discursive
reasoning. The Christian actionist contemplates the situation and
sees the answer.

Saint Thomas remarked that there was something superhu-
man about noësis. "The human soul, as far as concerns that
which is highest in it, touches on something which is proper to
the nature of the angels; that is to say, it acquires a knowledge
of some things suddenly and without investigation."[12] It is
through this ability that the contemplative person begins to understand the law of love. He sees the necessity of loving God
above all things because He is infinitely lovable. Then gradually
he understands that he must love his neighbor as himself because his neighbor reflects God's nature and shares His lovable-
ness.

It is hard to grasp the overwhelmingly important truth that
the personal qualities of one's neighbor do not constitute the essential ground for loving him. In the early days of modern social
work there used to be talk about "the worthy poor." The implication was that such people deserved help, but that there was no
real obligation to help the unworthy. This principle is quite
alien to the spirit of Christian charity. One day at the Capuchin
convent at Altötting in Bavaria a beggar came to the door and
asked the porter, Brother (now Saint) Conrad Birndorfer, for
some food. Brother Conrad explained that the good food was already exhausted, but he promised to do what he could. He managed to find a plate of soup. The beggar tasted it, found it not to

132

his liking, and smashed the plate angrily on the floor. Brother Conrad apologized, picked up the pieces of the broken dish, and went off to try again for something better. The saints loved the "unworthy" poor. This is of the essence of Christian charity. He who is to bear witness successfully must grasp this momentous fact.

It is essentially important that a Christian social-actionist project somehow preserve the spirit of contemplation. If the participating members lose sight of the essential reason for their work, then their project degenerates into mere philanthropy. They must not become so wrapped up in a round of activity that they do not have time for meditation and for thoughtful discussion. The essence of Christian social action is not *what* one does, but *why* one does it.

When the Christian actionist has attained clear insight into a problematic social situation and when he has judged it in the light of the New Testament moral code, there still remains the duty of proclaiming publicly what he has discovered. This, of course, is the essence of bearing witness.

There is a close relation between nonparticipation and bearing witness. When the personalist separates himself dramatically from the worldly community, he raises questions in the mind of the public. Why did this man burn his draft card? Why did these people leave their comfortable middle-class homes to take up residence in the slums? Curiosity is aroused. The public wants to know the answers. Then, too, the self-sacrifice of the nonparticipator creates a favorable atmosphere. His motives cannot be selfish. Of course, the man who is willing to die for his beliefs is the most convincing witness of all. "Martyr" is simply the Greek word for "witness." The martyr is the witness par excellence. But even minor sacrifices make an impression. They help give the message of the witness a stamp of authenticity.

The witness who believes deeply in the truth and importance of his message will proclaim it incessantly, under all circumstances. Saint Paul gave this advice to his disciple Timothy: "Preach the word. Be insistent in season and out of season."[13] The original Greek of the last phrase of this quotation would perhaps be better translated, "under both appropriate and inappropriate circumstances." The point was that Timothy should not hesitate to preach *akairōs,* that is, in a situation where the Hellenic ideal of good form, of moderation in all things, would demand silence.

The Christian witness preaches "in season." That is to say, he uses all the conventional publicity media to which he has access. If these is anything distinctive in his use of such media, it is a certain simplicity and directness. His prose is likely to be unornamented but very much to the point. The perfect model for this sort of exposition is furnished by the New Testament parables. They are simple stories. They are understandable even by the most simple; yet they have a depth of meaning which is fascinating to great minds.

The Christian witness also preaches "out of season." On Sunday, November 12, 1967, the Rev. C.P. Lewis, Rector of historic Burton Parish Church in Williamsburg, Virginia, found that the President of the United States was present in the congregation. Under the circumstances nothing could be more inappropriate than to embarrass the President by discussing the morality of the war in Vietnam; yet the Rector chose to do precisely that. He stated that "there is a general consensus that what we are doing in Vietnam is wrong." Moreover, he touched on the "credibility gap," a most sensitive point for the administration, when he called for a "logical, straightforward explanation" of Vietnam policy. Of course the Rector's bold action aroused a storm of protest. The Governor of Virginia apologized and Congressmen denounced the Rector.

If Christianity is to be socially effective, there must be an abundance of witnesses, both lay and clerical, who are willing to speak up "out of season." They must be willing to alienate persons in high places who might otherwise have been helpful to them. They must be willing to endure storms of criticism, name-calling, and the imputation of unworthy motives. It is only thus that the gospel message can become relevant. If one reduces that message to "a bland melange of inoffensive and uninteresting moral principles," than one will indeed escape criticism, but at the expense of abjuring the "responsibility to make the Gospel relevant to life."[14] Purchasing peace by reticence in order to avoid controversy is a very short-sighted policy.

NOTES TO CHAPTER IX

1 Jn. 1:7.
2 Jn. 3:11.
3 Jn. 8:18.
4 Acts 1:8.
5 Acts 2:32.
6 Acts 10:39.
7 Acts 26:22.
8 Slum children show up very poorly in school; their IQ's average far below those of children from the white-collar class. It is now known that the low IQ's of the slum children are not due to heredity, but to lack of intellectual stimulation during the preschool years. At the present writing a research project on this subject is being completed at the Bureau of Social Research of the Catholic University of America for the National Institute of Mental Health. An experimental group of thirty slum infants was selected together with a matched control group. The former were systematically stimulated between the ages of 15 and 36 months by tutors who visited their homes, whereas the control group was left alone. The results are being analyzed at the time of the present writing, but it is already clear that the tutored infants have on the average at least normal intelligence and that the control infants are slipping far behind intellectually.
9 Several studies carried out at our Bureau of Social Research have made very clear the difficulty of retraining unemployed school dropouts.

10 On this, see a dissertation directed by the present writer: George M. Putnam and Edna M. O'Hern, "The Status Significance of an Isolated Urban Dialect," supplement to *Language*, Vol. 31, No. 4, Part 2 (October-December, 1955).

11 Paul H. Furfey, "The Aristotelian and Thomistic Theories of Noësis" in *Three Theories of Society* (New York, Macmillan, 1937), Chap. 3.

12 Saint Thomas, De verit., Q. 16, A. 1, c.

13 2 Tim. 4:2.

14 John B. Sheerin, "Should the Church Speak Out?", *Washington Catholic Standard* (November 9, 1967), p. 7.

CHAPTER X

Nonviolence

WHEN THE Christian actionist has separated himself from the evil mores of a wordly society, when he has studied the problems of his community and the application to these problems of New Testament principles, when he has boldly borne witness in season and out of season, his task is still incomplete. He must act to remove or at least minimize the social evils which he has denounced. Indeed, this is his essential goal.

The Christian personalist can use all legitimate forms of social action, including the most conventional. He can agitate for good social legislation. He can encourage collective bargaining by labor unions. He can organize pressure for the improvement of schools, health agencies, law enforcement, and correctional institutions. He can lend his aid to all sorts of social agencies and help them to grow and increase their efficiency. All these activities are good. Yet there is another form of action more appropriate to the Christian, and that is nonviolence. Of course, it is not true that nonviolence is an exclusively Christian technique. Gandhi was strikingly successful with it in non-Christian India. Yet the fact remains that the theory of nonviolence fits easily into Christian ideology and that Christians have often used the method with extraordinarily happy results.

137

Nonviolence may be defined as "a generic category of actions and attitudes that deliberately abstain from using force and violence in situations to which they might be applied."[1] The last clause in this definition is important. Nonviolence implies more than the mere absence of physical force. Such force is not generally used in a political campaign; yet we do not call such a campaign nonviolent action. But if a group of pickets are roughed up by some bystanders and do not retaliate, the case is different. When one is attacked, it is natural to become angry and strike back. The absence of any retaliation, when it is to be expected, constitutes the essence of nonviolence.

It is clear that Jesus Christ taught an ethic of nonviolence. His words in the Sermon on the Mount are familiar. "Do not resist the evildoer; but if anyone strikes you on the right cheek, turn to him the other also."[2] "Love your enemies and pray for those who persecute you."[3] On one occasion there was a popular movement to make Jesus king. Of course this would have meant an armed revolt against the Roman power; naturally, he repudiated the idea.[4] Of course, the strongest proof of His policy of nonviolence was the Crucifixion. The supreme purpose of His life on earth, the redemption of mankind, was consummated not by violence, but by yielding to the violence of those who were His enemies.

Some may see in Christ's expulsion of the buyers and sellers from the Temple an example of His personal use of violence. But in this case the violence was merely symbolic. No one was injured. Jesus created a scene only to dramatize His disapproval of the commercialization of a sacred area. Again, when He said, "I have come not to bring peace, but a sword,"[5] He was not stating the purpose of His coming, but rather its inevitable sequel. The disturbances were not to be caused by the application of His doctrine; they were to be caused by the bad dispositions of worldly men reacting to this doctrine.

It would be a mistake to believe that Christianity means the repudiation of physical force under all circumstances. If a mad-

138

man goes berserk and begins to kill innocent people, common sense dictates that force must be used against him. In the Palestine of Christ's day Roman soldiers fulfilled the function of modern police. They kept public order. In the New Testament there is no suggestion that they should put down their arms and allow anarchy to prevail.

In the New Testament nonviolence is not prescribed as the proper and ordinary policy of civil authorities. To keep the peace, nonviolence is not a substitute for the ordinary agencies of law enforcement. Nonviolence is not prescribed as a universal principle, but as a characteristically Christian policy. The impact of Christianity on the social order is something special. It is to be a moral impact, and it is precisely for this moral impact that nonviolence is prescribed. Nonviolence is not to be the total foundation of the social order; but it is to be a characteristic Christian technique for modifying the social order.

Nonviolence takes various forms. The simplest is *nonresistance*. This is a literal acceptance of the principle of the Sermon on the Mount. "Do not resist the evildoer." It implies a lack of resistance to physical force, not from impotence, not from cowardice, but from the application of the law of universal love.

The martyrs furnish the perfect example of nonresistance. It is undoubtedly true that the early martyrs were principally responsible for the conversion of the Roman world to Christianity. What happened furnishes a most dramatic example of the power of nonresistance. On the one hand was the Roman Empire, very efficiently organized and dominating the whole civilized Western world. On the other hand were the Christians, "not many wise according to the flesh, not many powerful, not many of noble birth."[6] The Empire outlawed Christianity. It marshaled its enormous power to crush the new religion. Yet after three centuries of persecutions, after countless martyrs had shed their blood, it was Christianity that triumphed. The Empire was converted.

139

It is important to ask how it was that the persecution of the Christians led to the conversion of pagans. The full answer to this question is doubtless very complex psychologically. However, some insight into the process can be gained if it is considered essentially as a form of communication. The martyr communicates something to the pagan onlooker.

In the first place, the martyr communicates the intensity of his faith. One must believe in the gospel very fully and very sincerely if one is willing to die for it. Of course there is always the possibility that the martyr is merely a fanatic, urged on by irrational and unconscious motives. However, if he has been known in the past as a solid citizen and if his demeanor as he approaches his death is calm and not frenetic, the hypothesis of fanaticism seems ruled out. At the very least, the spectator's curiosity is aroused. He wants to know something about this doctrine which the martyr considers so valuable.

The martyr also communicates the fact that he does not hate those who put him to death. It is normal for a persecuted minority to fight back. Men resolve to sell their lives dearly. It is less terrible to be killed with a sword in one's hand than to surrender and to be tortured at leisure. Also, if a man is captured by force, it is normal for him to snarl at his captors, to show hatred towards them. The Christians did none of these things. They professed to love their persecutors; and their conduct was such that it was hard to believe that this love was at all insincere.

Finally the Christians communicated something to their persecutors' conscience. Most men have at least some vestigial sense of fairness, even though it is usually latent. It is hard to be deliberately cruel unless one can persuade oneself that the opponent is evil and deserves cruelty. A soldier can slaughter with a clear conscience if he can believe that his enemy is scarcely human and that intolerable damage will be done if he is allowed to survive. The conduct of the Christians was such that it was hard to maintain an image of them as evil. Therefore, an alter-

140

native possibility could force itself into the conscience of the persecutor. Perhaps the Christians were not evil, after all. Perhaps it was wrong to put them to death.

It is easy to see how ideas like these might gradually seep into the consciousness of the pagans. It was not a sudden process. It resulted in the conversion of individuals here and there, then of more and more persons. Gradually, a more favorable concept of Christianity took possession of public consciousness. When the Edict of Milan was promulgated in 313, the public was ready for it.

Martyrdom is the most striking example of the technique of nonresistance; however, it is by no means the only one. Suppose a group of actionists march in support of an open-housing ordinance. A gang of toughs attack them, but the marchers offer no resistance. They allow themselves to be kicked and beaten. They accept all sorts of verbal abuse. In a minor degree they are following the policy of the martyrs and the results are to some extent parallel. The fact that the marchers are willing to suffer in support of their position indicates the sincerity of their convictions. The unwillingness to counterattack means that they take the Sermon on the Mount seriously. In a moral sense, the attackers are thrown off balance. Their faith in their position is shaken. They begin to wonder whether there is something to be said for open housing, after all. It is clear that the technique of nonresistance has many possibilities.

A second form of nonviolent action is *passive resistance*. By this technique the actionist withdraws his cooperation from some activity involving his opponents. Strikes and boycotts are examples. Of course on such occasions violence may occur; but the passive resister does not allow himself to become involved in it. If attacked, he does not fight back. Nonviolent strikes and boycotts thus have a special quality.

Passive resistance was well illustrated by the Montgomery bus boycott. On December 1, 1955, Mrs. Rosa Parks refused to yield

141

her seat to a white passenger when ordered to do so by the bus driver. She was arrested as a result. Indignation spread rapidly through the Negro community and there was talk of attacking bus drivers and beating them up. However, calmer counsel prevailed and a very successful boycott was organized. Instead of traveling by bus, Negroes rode taxis, organized car pools, or walked to work. The boycott was very effective and lasted an entire year.

In the course of the boycott the segregationists tried intimidation. There were arrests on trumped-up charges. Leaders were insulted and threatened by anonymous letters and phone calls. The most dramatic attempts at intimidation were the three bombings of homes of boycott leaders. For example, on January 30, 1956, a bomb was exploded on the porch of Martin Luther King's home. Hundreds of angry Negroes gathered at the scene. It seemed that all the elements necessary for a riot were present. However, King succeeded in calming the crowd. "We must love our white brothers," he said, "no matter what they do to us." It was a most remarkable exhibition of nonviolence under most provocative circumstances.

On December 1, 1956, a decree of the Supreme Court overturned the city ordinance that prescribed segregation on the buses. The boycott then ceased. Of course, it was the court order, rather than the boycott itself, that ended segregation. However, the boycott did have a number of important effects. It stimulated bus boycotts elsewhere and led a number of southern cities to desegregate buses without court order. What was more important was the fact that the publicity coming from Montgomery made Negroes realize that it was possible to abolish long-standing segregationist practices through well-organized nonviolent action.

An example of a quite different sort of passive resistance was the strike at the Catholic University of America in April 1967 over the dismissal of Father Charles E. Curran without a hearing and indeed without any explanation at all. After his dismissal had been announced, Father Curran's colleagues in the School of Sacred Theology met on April 19 and unanimously passed a resolution declaring: "We can not and will not function until Father Curran is reinstated." The next day the entire full-time faculty of the University met and also voted, 400 to 18, to strike. The student body joined in and all University activities were suspended. There were prayer vigils, picket lines, and mass meetings. Throughout the strike a spirit of calm and peace prevailed. There was no name-calling, no insults against the authorities. Finally, on April 24, the administration yielded. Father Curran was retained on the faculty and also promoted. The strike was very successful indeed; it not only attained its immediate objective but also stimulated a movement to reorganize and modernize the administrative structure of the University.

Passive resistance goes a bit further than nonresistance. It takes the positive step of frustrating the opponents' activities through noncooperation. Whereas nonresistance can create a generally favorable impression, as when the heroism of the martyrs impressed the pagans, passive resistance can be directed toward a specific objective, toward the desegregation of buses or the reinstatement of a faculty member.

The most difficult, and at the same time the most widely effective, form of nonviolence is *nonviolent direct action.* In passive resistance the actionist merely withdraws his cooperation. In nonviolent direct action he takes the tactical offensive. He moves into the disputed area and disrupts activities there. A classical example is furnished by the sit-ins of 1960.

On February 1, 1960, four colored students from Shaw University, Greensboro, North Carolina, sat down at a lunch counter in a local Woolworth store that had been reserved for white customers. They were refused service, but they continued to sit. Day after day more students came and maintained the sit-in. The movement spread rapidly to other cities. Often white students joined in.

Segregationist opposition to the sit-ins took various forms. Demonstrators were attacked with axe handles and baseball bats or sprayed with insecticide. Girls' hair was pulled. There was heckling. Insults were shouted. Marches to back up the sit-ins were attacked with tear-gas bombs and fire hoses; marchers were arrested. All these tactics were met with nonviolence.

In general the sit-ins were strikingly successful. The underlying reason for this success was economic. Not only did merchants lose revenue from their lunch counters, but the unsettled conditions created in the shopping district by the demonstrations kept business away. Beside attaining their immediate objective, the sit-ins had a good general effect on interracial relations. The contrast between the ugly tactics of the white troublemakers and the calm courage of the demonstrators was not lost on the American public. The sit-ins proved the effectiveness of nonviolence.

The freedom rides of 1961 were another very striking demonstration of the power of nonviolent direct action. The first of these freedom rides left Washington, D.C., on May 14, heading for New Orleans. The riders were six Negro-white pairs. At each stop segregated facilities were tested. For example, a Negro rider would sit at a lunch counter reserved for whites. At first all went smoothly. However, at Rock Hill, South Carolina, the riders were attacked by hoodlums. There were other incidents, but the climax was at Anniston, Alabama. Here a mob set the bus on fire with an incendiary bomb and beat up several of the freedom riders. The injured were treated at a hospital and then taken to Birmingham by car. The other riders left for Birmingham on another bus. On arriving there, the freedom riders were again attacked by a mob and one of them, Jim Peck, was very badly beaten. It was nevertheless planned to resume the ride the next day. However, the bus drivers refused to take the freedom riders; and the plans had to be canceled.

A group of students from Nashville resolved to continue the

freedom ride from Birmingham to New Orleans. They succeeded in getting as far as Montgomery, but there they were met by a mob of hundreds of persons. The riders were attacked and injured. Local police seemed unable to control the mob and the Governor would not call out the National Guard. Finally the Federal Government sent several hundred U.S. marshals to the spot and they proved helpful. In the meantime, however, it was announced that Martin Luther King was planning a rally in support of the freedom riders at a local church. A mob converged on the church and it was so large and unruly that the marshals were unable to cope with it. The Governor was finally forced to call out the National Guard to restore peace.

These two freedom rides were followed by many others. They were marked by some disorders, arrests, and jailings. However, by the end of the summer, the movement had made its point. Public opinion had been aroused and the government had to act. The Interstate Commerce Commission issued new regulations on interstate travel. From November 1 on, interstate buses had to display a sign: "Seating aboard this vehicle without regard to race, color, creed or national origin, by order of the Interstate Commerce Commission." The same policy of integration was enforced in terminals involved in interstate travel.

It is interesting to note that nonviolent direct action can obtain its objectives in various different ways. The sit-ins used economic pressure to force the desegregation of lunch counters. However, in the case of the freedom rides there was practically no economic pressure at all. In this instance the desired result was obtained by arousing public opinion which moved the Federal Government to act.

The preceding examples of nonviolent action give only an inadequate idea of what is actually a very complex subject. Nonviolence implies first of all a special philosophy of life. For the Christian this philosophy is simply deduced from the law of

145

love which is the ethical core of the New Testament. It is the philosophy expressed so beautifully in the Sermon on the Mount.

In addition, there are many practical matters which must be settled before nonviolence can be used successfully. An organization must be formed and leaders must be trained. Then an appropriate strategy must be selected, for, as has been made clear above, nonviolence takes various forms. Then there are endless details. How does one dress for a sit-in? How can one best protect oneself from injury if attacked? What are one's rights after arrest? The actionist must know the answers to many such questions if he is to act efficiently.[7]

In spite of the intrinsic difficulties of the technique, there is much to be said in favor of a wider use of nonviolence. This is particularly true in a democracy where public opinion can influence governmental policy; nonviolence generally makes a good impression and thus moves opinion in a favorable direction. Then, too, nonviolence is sanctifying. It demands self-sacrifice for the sake of others. It is thus a very active and pure form of charity.

Nonparticipation, bearing witness, and nonviolence are three action techniques which are particularly appropriate for the Christian actionist. Of course, he will use other worthy methods when they are called for and he will use them together with all men of good will. Thus he may agitate for good social legislation or campaign for worthy candidates for public office. However, for his own distinctively Christian social action, the three techniques mentioned are especially suitable.

By nonparticipation the actionist separates himself sharply from the evil mores of a worldly society; doing so may even involve disobedience to unjust laws. Then he carefully studies the social realities around him, judges them in the light of the Authentic Code of Christian love, and bears witness to what he has discovered. Finally, he finds nonviolence to be a very effective

146

way of bringing about changes that eliminate social evil and build a holy society.

Let it be emphasized once more that social action of some sort is the duty of every Christian. It is not a work of supererogation, but an obligation binding in conscience. The exact nature of this duty on any specific occasion depends on one's abilities and on the circumstances. Sometimes one must act alone, sometimes as a member of a personalist group. But act one must in some way. That is a fundamental Christian duty.

NOTES TO CHAPTER X

1 William R. Miller, *Nonviolence: a Christian Interpretation* (New York, Association Press, 1964), p. 367.
2 Mt. 5:39. The Greek text might be equally well translated, "Do not resist evil," or "Do not resist the Evil One." However, "Do not resist the evildoer," seems to fit the context better.
3 Mt. 5:44. The Douay Version translates this: "Love your enemies: do good to them that hate you: and pray for them that persecute and calumniate you." However, the additional words on which this longer translation is based are missing in the best Greek texts.
4 Jn. 6:15.
5 Mt. 10:34.
6 1 Cor. 1:32.
7 The following offer good discussions of techniques: Martin Oppenheimer and George Lakey, *A Manual for Direct Action* (Chicago, Quadrangle Books, 1965), and Miller, "The Dynamics of Nonviolence," *op. cit.,* pp. 131-214.

Index